A CRASH COURSE IN
COOL TRICKS

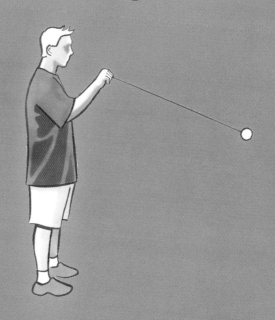

A CRASH COURSE IN
COOL TRICKS

Ed Riley and Dan Morgan

METRO BOOKS
NEW YORK

Illustrations by: Pat Murray
Authors: Ed Riley and Dan Morgan

Metro Books
122 Fifth Avenue
New York, NY 10011

ISBN-13: 978-1-4351-0754-0
ISBN-10: 1-4351-0754-3

Printed and bound in China

1 3 5 7 9 10 8 6 4 2

The whole point of this book is to learn some new skills and to have fun while doing so, but it is always wise to make sure that you are safe at the same time.

Some of the tricks and skills in *A Crash Course In Cool Tricks* can be dangerous to perform so you *must* take all due care and precautions when learning and performing them:

- Always master the basic skills before attempting more advanced tricks.

- Always wear any appropriate safety gear and protective clothing.

- Always ensure that you have ample room to practise and perform the tricks.

- If you are at all unsure about your ability to perform any of the tricks or skills, you should not attempt to do so.

- As well as your own safety, always consider the safety of others when you perform any of the tricks or skills.

CONTENTS

SKATEBOARDING

SKATEBOARDING HAS COME A LONG WAY FROM ITS HUMBLE BEGINNINGS IN THE 1950S' SURFING CRAZE IN THE U.S. WHEN BOARDS WERE SIMPLY A PIECE OF TWO BY FOUR WITH ROLLER SKATE WHEELS ATTACHED. RIDERS DISCOVERED THAT THE SENSATION OF SURFING WAVES COULD BE RECREATED ON DRY LAND.

Today, largely through the sponsorship of big business, skating is an internationally recognized sport and a multi-billion dollar industry, with the skaters themselves becoming household names. Image is everything; skateboard companies make more money from selling shoes and clothing than they do the boards themselves.

Street skating, where existing urban structures are used to perform tricks and maneuvers has emerged as the most popular form of the activity and where most professional skaters cut their teeth.

Skateboards continue to evolve technically but there have been several notable innovations that have shaped them visually and influenced way they are ridden:

• **Wheels and trucks:** Early in board development, steering was made easier by allowing the board to pivot left and right on its axles, effectively turning the wheels. Urethane wheels, invented in the 1970s, provide surface grip and speed. Wheel size has increased over the years.

- **The kicktail:** Arguably the most important development to come to the sport. A raised edge added to the rear made possible many of the tricks that are the staple of present day riders' repertoires. A front kicktail pushed the possibilities of freestyle skateboarding still further.

As a newcomer to the sport you need to look after yourself, so here are a few useful safety tips:

- **Use protection!** You are going to fall off. A lot. Loose clothing, knee pads, elbow pads and helmet are a must.
- **Learn in a purpose built skate park;** somewhere the urban environment has been recreated and there are other skaters to help you out if you get into trouble.
- **Try not to fall fowl of the law,** skating is considered a danger to the public in many places and you may find yourself in hot water. Increasingly, "skate stoppers"—devices that prevent civic instalations being used for tricks—are being installed in urban areas.

FAMOUS SKATEBOARDERS:

Stacy Peralta—now a film and TV director, often credited with popularizing skateboarding during the 1970s.

Tony Hawk—the most recognizable face in skateboarding and star of numerous films and computer games and inventor of countless tricks.

Jason Lee—pro skater turned international film star, can currently be seen in the U.S. sitcom My Name is Earl.

OLLIE

① Push off on your right foot to give yourself some momentum

② and ③ Once you are moving place your right foot on the tail of the board and your left foot just behind the front wheels (the majority of your weight should be on your left foot)

④ Crouch down to prepare your jump

⑤ Push down and jump up off both feet

⑥ and ⑦ The tail of the board should strike the ground, causing the front to rise up

⑧ Drag your left foot up the board

⑨ The board will now start to level off

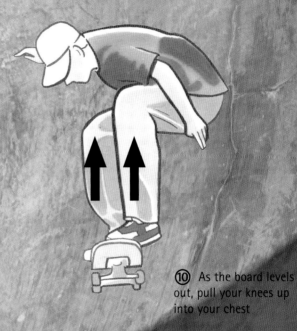

⑩ As the board levels out, pull your knees up into your chest

11 and **12** Once you reach the apex of your jump gently push down your legs

13 and **14** As you land bend your knees to absorb the impact

KICK FLIP

① Set off as you would for an Ollie, but with your right foot

② and ③ As you take off drag your left foot *across* the board diagonally, flipping it with your toes

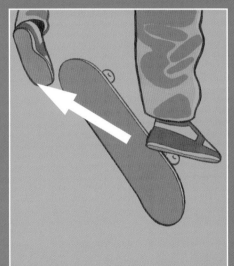

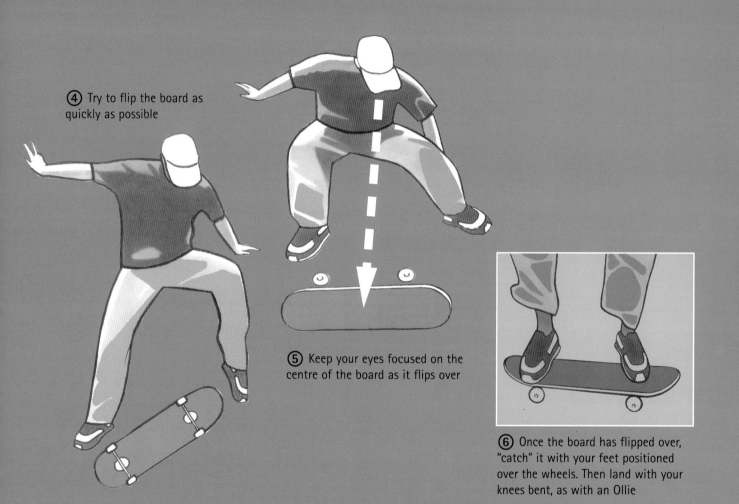

④ Try to flip the board as quickly as possible

⑤ Keep your eyes focused on the centre of the board as it flips over

⑥ Once the board has flipped over, "catch" it with your feet positioned over the wheels. Then land with your knees bent, as with an Ollie

HEEL FLIP

① and ② Set your feet the same as for an Ollie or a Kick Flip, but with your left foot further across the board

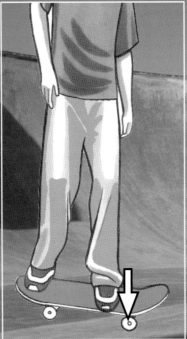

③ As you take off kick your left foot diagonally across the board, flipping it with your heel

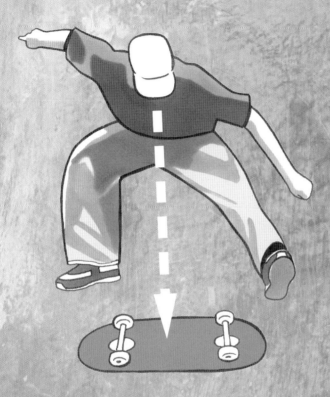

④ and ⑤ Once the board has flipped over, "catch" it with your feet positioned over the wheels. Then land with your knees bent, as with an Ollie

GRINDING - 50/50

① Build up your speed and keep the board parallel to the rail as you approach

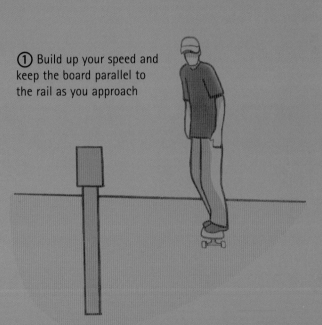

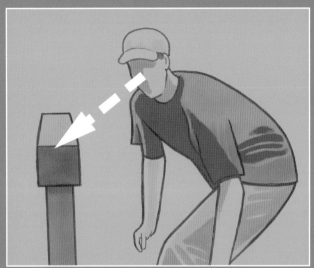

② Focus your eyes on the part of the rail you are aiming to jump onto

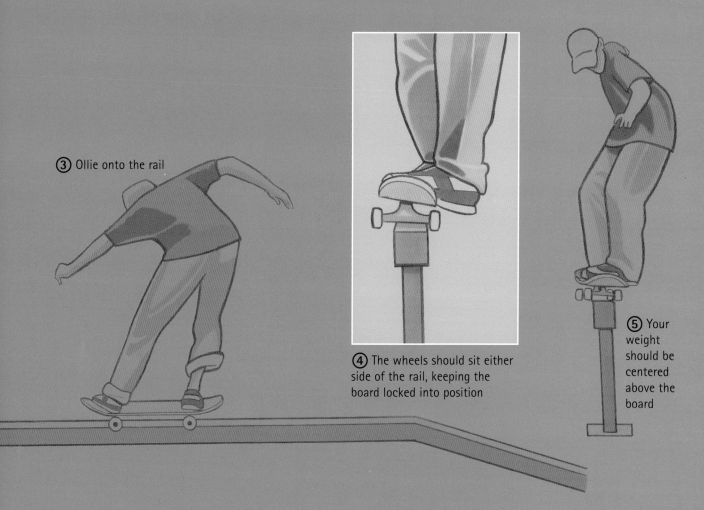

③ Ollie onto the rail

④ The wheels should sit either side of the rail, keeping the board locked into position

⑤ Your weight should be centered above the board

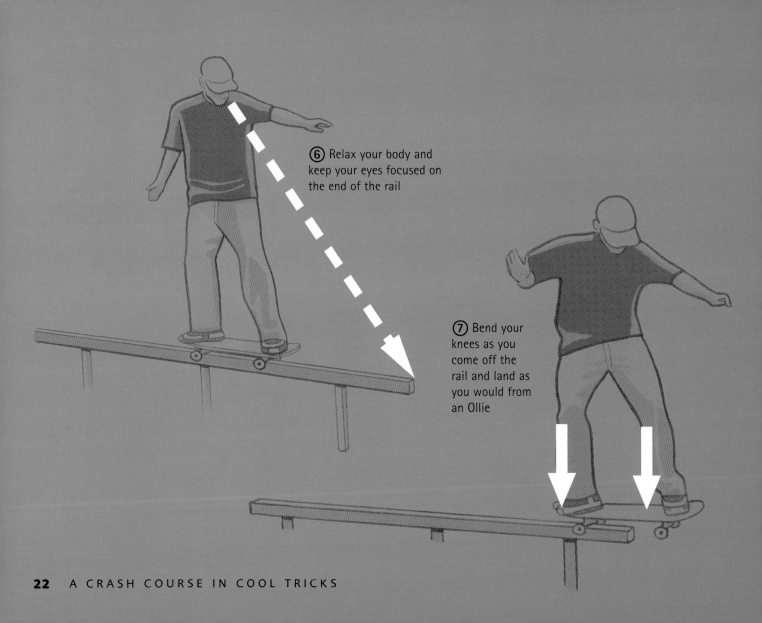

⑥ Relax your body and keep your eyes focused on the end of the rail

⑦ Bend your knees as you come off the rail and land as you would from an Ollie

GRINDING - BOARD SLIDE

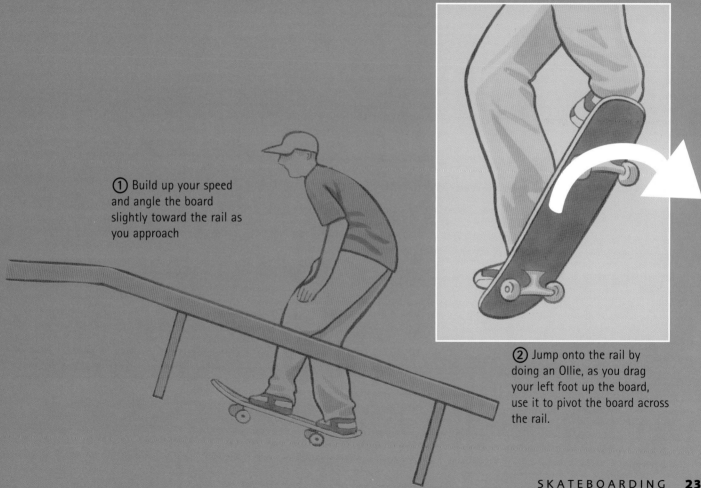

① Build up your speed and angle the board slightly toward the rail as you approach

② Jump onto the rail by doing an Ollie, as you drag your left foot up the board, use it to pivot the board across the rail.

③ As your left foot comes across the rail, swing your left arm forward so that it acts as a counterbalance

④ Aim to land with your weight centered directly above the rail

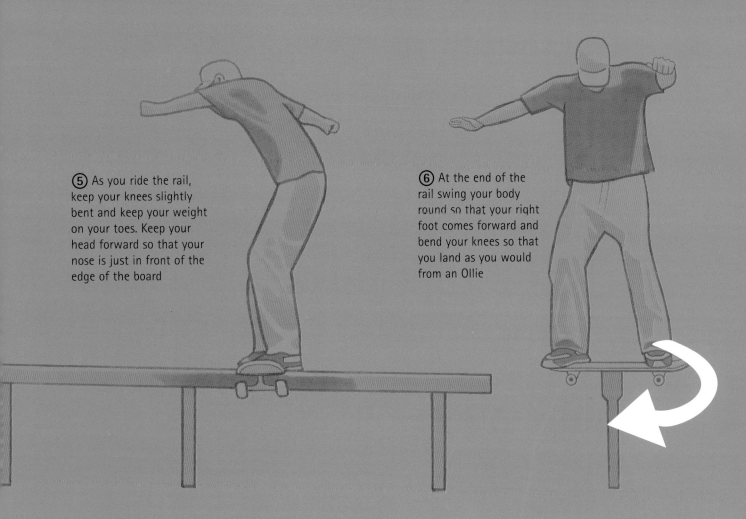

⑤ As you ride the rail, keep your knees slightly bent and keep your weight on your toes. Keep your head forward so that your nose is just in front of the edge of the board

⑥ At the end of the rail swing your body round so that your right foot comes forward and bend your knees so that you land as you would from an Ollie

BASKETBALL

BASKETBALL, ONE OF THE WORLD'S MOST POPULAR SPORTS, SCARCELY NEEDS ANY INTRODUCTION. DESPITE BEING HUGE IN THE U.S. WHERE THE SPORT WAS INVENTED, BASKETBALL HAS MADE GLOBAL SUPERSTARS OF ITS PLAYERS, EVEN IN COUNTRIES WHERE IT IS LESS POPULAR.

The brainchild of Canadian Dr James Naismith, basketball met a need for a game that could be played indoors during winter months and, due to the confines this imposed, did not rely on brute strength alone. The rules are such that using physical force to obtain the ball will result in a foul and changes in possession must occur while the ball is in motion. From its inception in 1891, the game was played using soccer balls (basketballs as we know them today did not exist) with points being scored by shooting into peach baskets.

Basketball is interesting from the point of view that to play the game well, tricks must be learned—rather than being merely an amusing aside from the game itself, all in the name of preventing your opponent getting hold of the ball.

Worldwide, no team is as well known as the legendary Harlem Globetrotters, who mainly play exhibition matches during which players are able to show off their considerable aptitude for tricks. As their name suggests, the Globetrotters see a fair bit of the world and have developed routines (often comedic) to wow crowds. Despite this, the Globetrotters consider themselves a serious team and frequently take part in professional games.

An international competition, the FIBA (International Basketball Federation) World Championship occurs every four years and in 2006 was held in Japan. The tournament featured 24 national teams and was eventually won by Spain.

Fancy footwork and dribbling skills are doubtless vital elements of any player's game. But to really impress, work on your shooting. Some positions may do more scoring than others, but every player must be able to place the ball in the basket when an opportunity presents itself. Michael Jordan, basketball's most celebrated player, is regarded as a superb all-rounder but it was his endless shooting practice, or drill, that enabled him to become such a prolific scorer.

There are five basic player positions in basketball:

- **Point guard** – usually a team's best dribbler and passer, directs the offense.
- **Shooting guard** – similar to point guard except does not usually drive the ball forward. Relied on to score "jump-shots" (long baskets from the perimeter area).
- **Small forward** – the primary point scorer, the small forward uses their athleticism to evade opposing players and steal the ball.
- **Power forward** – usually physically larger than the other players, primarily used in defense.
- **Center** – usually the tallest players on the court, vital to both offense and defense.

SPINNING THE BALL

① Cup the ball in your left hand and hold it at head height, with your right hand resting on the back of the ball

② Start the ball spinning by swiftly rolling your right hand across the side of the ball, flick your wrist as you do this to generate as much spin as possible

③ Keep your eyes on the ball

④ Catch the ball on the index finger of your left hand

⑤ Keep the ball spinning by swiftly rolling your right hand across the side of the ball, flick your wrist as you do this to generate as much spin as possible

⑥ Keep your eyes focused on the ball and repeat step five

CROSSOVER

① Keep your weight on your left foot and step forward with your right foot

② Change your direction by bringing your right foot forward *across* your body

③ Keep the ball behind your leg, so that both your calf and your right hand guard it

④ To go the other way, keep your weight on your right foot and step forward with your left foot

⑤ Change your direction by bringing your left foot forward across your body

⑥ Move forward with the ball and finish as in image three, with the ball behind your leg, so that both your calf and your left hand guard it

FREE THROW

① Relax your body and stand with your feet parallel (roughly shoulders width apart), toes pointing toward the basket

② Keep your eyes focused on the basket

③ Hold the ball in the palm of your right hand, with your left hand on the side of the ball

④ When you are set throw the ball up, towards the basket

⑥ Follow through the throw so that your right arm comes up straight beside your head

⑤ As you release the ball keep your eyes focused on the basket

FREE THROW DRILL

① Use these two fingers and your thumb to throw the ball, this will keep the trajectory straight

② Start with your arm bent and the ball held just above your head. Your head should be tilted back and your eyes focused on an imaginary target above you

③ Throw the ball directly up, imparting spin with your thumb and the two fingers shown in image one

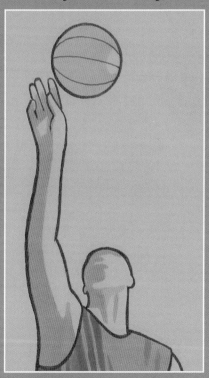

④ Follow through the throw so that your arm straightens

⑤ Keep your eyes on the ball

⑥ Catch the ball in the same position that you started the throw

UNDERHAND FREE THROW

① Relax your body and stand with your feet parallel (roughly shoulders width apart), toes pointing toward the basket.

② Focus your eyes on a spot just above the center of the basket

③ Bend your knees slightly and bring the ball down so that it is level with your crotch

④ Straighten your legs and bring your arms up, roll your hands across the top of the ball

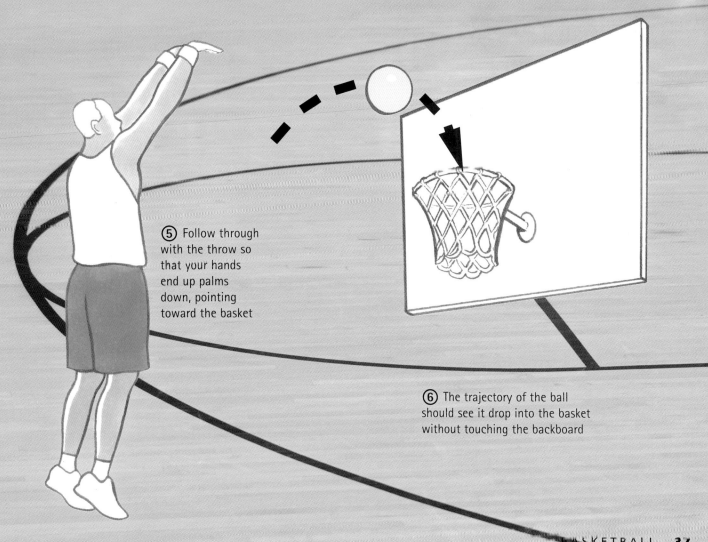

⑤ Follow through with the throw so that your hands end up palms down, pointing toward the basket

⑥ The trajectory of the ball should see it drop into the basket without touching the backboard

⚽ SOCCER

FREESTYLE SOCCER IS AN EXTENSION OF THE SKILLS AN ATHLETE MUST POSSESS FOR NORMAL TEAM PLAY THOUGH THE TWO DISCIPLINES COMPLEMENT EACH OTHER. A PLAYER DEVELOPING THEIR FREESTYLE SKILLS WILL NOTICE AN IMPROVEMENT IN THEIR TEAM GAME; BETTER COORDINATION AND BALL CONTROL, IN ADDITION TO IMPROVED PERCEPTION OF THE BALL'S BEHAVIOR—KNOWN AS GETTING A "FEEL" FOR THE BALL. THE REACH OF THIS DISCIPLINE EXTENDS TO AUDIENCES WHO ARE NOT FANS OF LEAGUE SOCCER.

Dubbed the world's most popular game, history tells us that soccer has its roots as far back 50BC, with something resembling the game being played between teams from China and Japan. However, soccer (or association football) as we know it today originated in the United Kingdom, becoming popular during the eighth century. In fact, you will often hear an Englishman complaining, whenever an international game is lost, how bitterly unfair it is that despite his country inventing the game, it does not win every match.

Soccer is truly a global game, with a country's indigenous team often featuring an line-up of international stars. The FIFA (Fédération Internationale de Football Association) World Cup is the most watched event of any in the sporting calendar. The tournament takes place every four years. Around 284 million people watched the final in 2006, during which Italy beat France and claimed their fourth trophy.

As an aside from the organized side of professional soccer, freestyling offers endless entertainment value, where international reputation is not necessarily at stake, as it is during a major competition. Demonstration events offer an ideal opportunity for soccer's corporate sponsors to showcase their players and the products that those individuals endorse. Television advertizements frequently feature big name players demonstrating freestyle skills, while the advent of video streaming on the internet has allowed unknowns to showcase their otherwise unseen talents to a mass audience. It is generally acknowledged that global advertising campaigns have driven the take up of freestyle soccer.

Freestyling can be practiced alone and with the minimum of equipment (a soccer ball). All you need is some (preferably outdoor) space and the inclination. Freestyling requires A LOT of practice. Start off by perfecting basic moves for it is these that form the foundations of more difficult maneuvers. Achieving a little at a time will deliver the drive and determination to learn ever more complex tricks, enabling you to bask in the adoration of your fans.

FREESTYLERS OF NOTE:

Steve 'Eli Freeze' Alias (Canada)—crowned Red Bull "King of All Freestylers", New York, U.S. 2007.
John Farnworth (UK)—currently holds the world record for around the worlds (ATWs) at 83 completed in one minute.

FLIP UPS - BACK & BEHIND

① and ② Drag the ball back with your right foot

④ and ⑤ and ⑥ When the ball reaches your left foot, raise your foot and flip the ball into the air

③ Place your right foot back on the ground

FLIP UPS - PULL & FLICK

① Drag the ball back with your left foot

② As the ball comes back move your right foot forward

③ and ④ Flick the ball up with your toes

FLIP UPS – SLAP SAME TIME

① Place your feet either side of the ball (with the center of the ball level with your instep)

② Quickly bring your feet together

③ The ball jumps up automatically

FLIP UPS - ROLL & FLICK

① Place the ball between your feet (with the center of the ball level with your ankles)

② Shift your weight to your left foot

③ With your right foot drag the ball up your left leg and roll it over your ankle

④ As the ball passes your left ankle jump up off your left foot

⑤ and ⑥ As the ball rolls down onto your left foot flip it up into the air

ROUND THE WORLD

BEFORE STARTING ENSURE THAT YOU HAVE THE BALL
UNDER CONTROL AND THAT YOUR HEAD AND CHEST
ARE POINTING TOWARD THE CENTER OF THE BALL

① Relax your
body and lift the
ball on your right
foot (keeping your
foot in contact
with the ball)

② Flick the ball
up so that it
rises to roughly
crotch level and
move your foot
out from under
the ball

③ and ④ and ⑤
Swing your right leg
around the ball

6 Catch and control the ball back on the top of your right foot

FLYING KICK

① Begin by juggling the ball between your two feet

② When you are in control of the ball kick the ball up with your right leg

③ Jump up off your left leg

④ and ⑤ The ball should reach the apex of its flight about twelve inches above your head. Your left foot should now be firmly back on the ground and you should begin to move your right leg upward

⑥ Hold your arms out to improve your balance

⑦ As the ball begins to drop jump up off your left leg

⑧ Bring your right
leg round and over
the ball

⑨ and ⑩ Bring your left
foot up and kick the ball
with the inside of your foot

FRISBEE

MANY HAVE CLAIMED TO BE HAVE INVENTED THE EVER POPULAR
FLYING DISC, BUT THE MOST LIKELY EXPLANATION SEEMS TO BE THE
DISCOVERY THAT "FLINGING" THE TIN PIE CASINGS USED BY THE
FRISBIE BAKING COMPANY (U.S.) FROM ONE PERSON TO ANOTHER,
MADE AN EXCELLENT PASTIME.

By the middle of the 20th century, the "Frisbee" had gone from pie tin to toy. Perhaps the most famous name in Frisbee history is Ed Headrick, former general manager for U.S. toy maker Wham-O who patented a design in 1964 which has sold tens of millions of units worldwide.

Headrick went on to invent "Disc Golf", which is played in a similar way to the game involving balls, clubs and 18 holes and enjoyed by millions of people internationally culminating in the PDGA (Professional Disc Golf Association) Player's Cup. The flipside to this refined sport is Freestyle Frisbee, a natural development of the simple activity of throwing the disc between players and which is again very popular at competition level.

Play a game of Frisbee that involves doing anything more than merely catching the disc and you may find yourself in a "Jam". "Jamming"—so called because the activity is conducted in an unrehearsed manner, similar to musicians performing an impromptu session—can take place between any number of participants. Each takes their turn to execute as many maneuvers as possible before passing the disc on to the next player.

Freestyle Frisbee is currently enjoying a surge in popularity, particularly in Europe. In addition to "Jamming", freestyle competitions also include events similar to figure skating; where teams of two or three players perform a routine to music and are judged on technical skill and style. As you may imagine, freestyle competitions are usually held outdoors, so wind conditions are an important and unpredictable factor during play.

Freestyle Frisbee players often make use of a false nail, temporarily fixed over their own, to aid in spinning the disc. Devices are also attached to the feet to facilitate "Toejam" where a Frisbee is balanced on the player's shoe or toenail. Silicon spray can be applied to the underside of the disc to allow it to spin for longer.

Successful Freestyle Frisbee:

- "Jam" in plenty of open space, preferably not where you are likely to trip over families trying to enjoy a picnic.
- Look out for dangers nearby such as electricity pylons and open water.
- Ideal wind speed is between three and six miles an hour (a light breeze).
- Frisbee is not generally a dangerous sport, but limber up as you would before any athletic activity to avoid muscle strain.

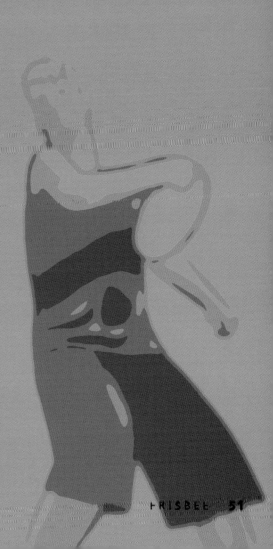

BODY ROLL

② Spin the frisbee from your right hand across your body to just above your outstretched left hand

③ Catch the frisbee on your left hand and it will spin down your hand along your arm

① Face into the wind and spread your arms out to provide a flat surface for the frisbee to travel across

4 and **5** Lean slightly backward to provide as flat a surface as possible for the frisbee to travel across

6 Catch and hold the frisbee as it arrives back in your right hand

AIRBOUNCE THROW

WITH THIS THROW THE FRISBEE WILL BEGIN
ITS FLIGHT HEADING DOWNWARD AND THEN
RISE UP HALF WAY THROUGH

① Take your normal backhand grip on the frisbee and stand side on

② and ③ Lift your right foot as you pull the frisbee back

④ Bring your right leg down as you bring the frisbee forward

⑤ Push against the ground with your right leg to give added momentum to the frisbee

⑥ Aim the frisbee down toward the ground and tilt it up slightly just before you release it

⑦ Flick your right wrist as you release the frisbee

⑧ Follow through with your right arm so that it ends up behind your back

OVERHAND WRIST FLICK

① Hold the frisbee with three fingers on top and your index finger along the edge

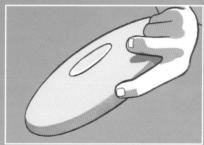

④ Stand side on

② Your thumb should sit on the inside rim of the frisbee

③ As you draw your arm back, your wrist should be angled back

⑤ Your arm should be straight at the back of the throw

⑥ As you bring the frisbee forward open your shoulders and move your weight onto your right foot

⑦ Lean slightly to the left as you come forward to help flatten the frisbee

⑧ Ensure that the frisbee is fully horizontal when you release it

⑨ Flick your wrist as you release the frisbee to impart spin to your throw

THUMBER

① Hold the frisbee upside down with your thumb on the inside rim

② Hold your four fingers together on the top of the frisbee

④ and ⑤ Keep your left arm straight as you move forward

③ Lean back so that the frisbee is pointing upward

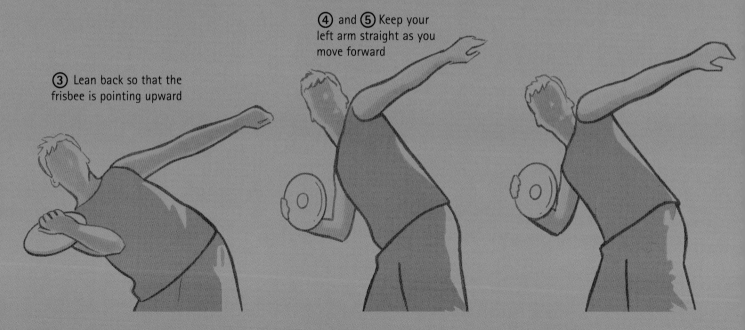

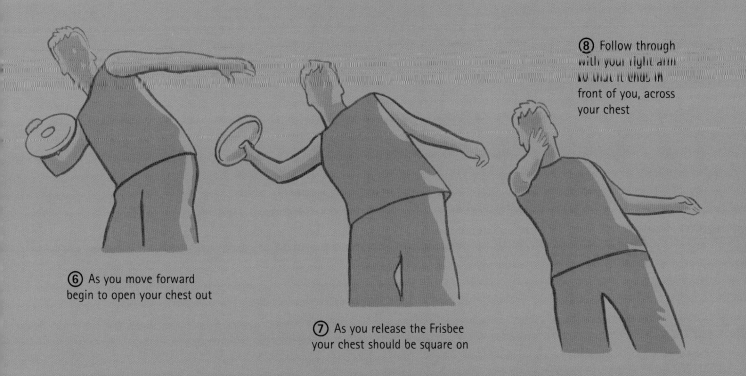

⑧ Follow through with your right arm so that it ends in front of you, across your chest

⑥ As you move forward begin to open your chest out

⑦ As you release the Frisbee your chest should be square on

FLICK

① Hold your index finger and your middle finger in a V on the underside of the frisbee

② and ③ Your thumb should sit on top of the frisbee with your last two fingers held against the palm of your hand.

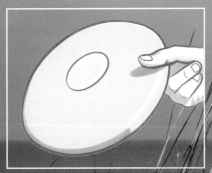

④ Stand side on

(5) As you draw the frisbee back, lean back to add power to your throw

(6) Tilt the frisbee so that it is pointing upward to avoid throwing it into the ground

⑦ and ⑧ Flick the frisbee with your middle
finger as you release it to add momentum to
your throw

9 and **10** and **11** Your right arm should follow through from the flick so that it ends up back behind you.

ROPES & WHIPS

Probably introduced to the United States from Spain, the bull whip is so called from the days it was used as a device to drive cattle through the Old West, and to deal with uncooperative bulls, trying to protect their harem of cows. Though it is often claimed that bull whips were not intended to actually strike cattle, the noise would certainly have got their attention.

Today whip cracking has evolved into competitions that take place all over the world. Indeed, the annual United Kingdom Whipcracking Convention is now into its fourth year, while in Australia whip cracking remains a perennial favorite.

When whip cracking, it pays to be over cautious, you really could take someone's eye out with that!

- Use eye protection.
- Wear clothes that will help to absorb the impact should the whip strike your body. Jeans are good, leather is better. Cover exposed flesh.

- If whip cracking for long periods, consider ear defenders.
- Make sure there is no-one within twenty feet of you.

Roping is the "Yin" to the bull whip's "Yang". While the whip was used to drive cattle forward, lassoing was required to capture or rescue as necessary. The word lasso describes the act of roping an object or animal, not the rope itself which is known as a "lariat". Especially common in rodeo competitions, roping remains extremely popular in the United States. Most events are conducted solo except team roping, in which two ropers on horseback must ensnare and tie a steer in the fastest time possible.

A good quality rope that will resist unraveling during repeated use is required for creating the lariat. A lariat is created by passing one end of the rope through a knotted loop at the other, known as a "Honda". Once through the Honda, the free end of the rope becomes the "Spoke" which is then used to manipulate the lariat.

As with whip cracking, considerable personal space is required for lasso practice so do it outside. The arm you use for this activity is going to get very tired, so warm up properly first. Most importantly, remember that showing off your skills by lassoing family and friends will win you no favors.

HOW TO CRACK A WHIP

① Mentally aim the whip at an object in the distance and start to swing your arm up

② Ensure that the motion of your arm is quick and fluid, *not* jerky

③ The whip should remain fully extended as you draw it back

④ Your hand should end up above your shoulder, level with your head; your elbow should be pointing toward your target. Cock your wrist backward

⑤ As the tip of the whip begins to drop behind you step forward on your left leg and begin to bring the whip forward

⑥ Keep your thumb on top of the whip handle and snap your wrist forward as you bring the whip down. The loop that this creates is vital as it is this that causes the whip to crack

⑦ End your forward swing with your arm out straight. Do *not* bring your arm lower than this as it will cause the whip to hit the ground

ONE BEHIND & ONE IN FRONT

② When your right hand is level with your head begin to bring the whip down

③ Bring the whip down in a semi-circular motion so that the tip of the whip hits the ground level with your feet

① Bring the whip up behind you

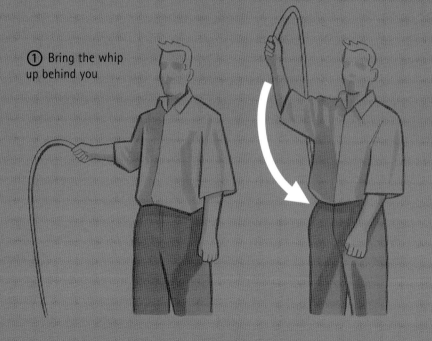

④ Bring the whip back up so that it arcs over your right shoulder

⑤ and ⑥ Just before the tip of the whip hits the ground behind you, bring the whip forward over your shoulder

⑦ The tip of the whip should hit the ground roughly one meter in front of you

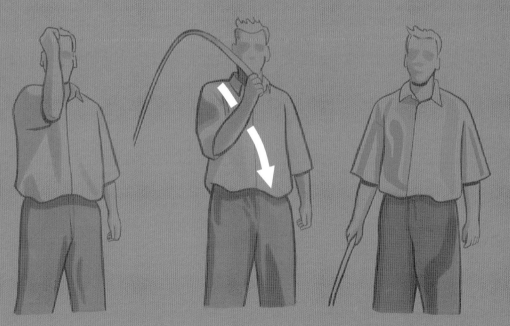

KILL THE SNAKE

① Bring the whip up behind you

② Bring the whip down, with your wrist moving in a circular motion

③ The tip of the whip should hit the ground one to two meters in front of you

④ and ⑤ Bring the whip back up so
that it comes back over your left shoulder.
Repeat these five steps a number of times

LASSOING

① Hold the Honda in your right hand and the rest of the rope in your left hand. Create a loop by feeding the rope through the Honda

② and ③ When the loop reaches roughly to your ankles, hold the top of the loop and the Honda in your right hand and use your left hand to pull the loop along the rest of the rope

⑤ Start with the loop held at your side, your right hand held at roughly shoulder height

⑥ Swing your right arm round, keeping your wrist straight

④ When the doubled up length of rope (known as the Spoke) is roughly a quarter of the way round the loop hold the rope in place with your left hand and slide your right hand along the rope so that you are holding it at the top of the spoke and the Honda is roughly half way down the loop

⑦ and ⑧ and ⑨ and ⑩ As the rope passes in front of you spin your wrist round so that your thumb goes from being at the top of your hand to the bottom

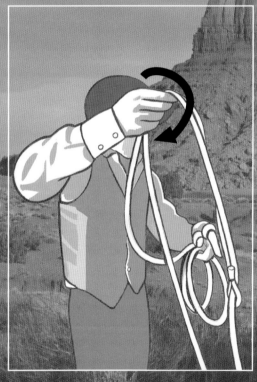

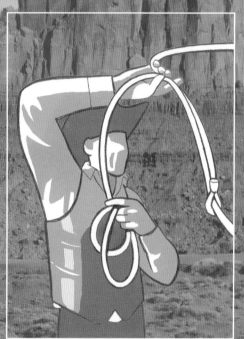

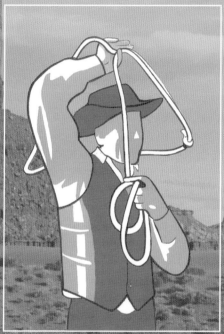

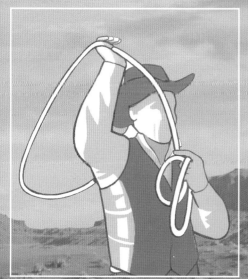

11 Continue to swing the rope around your head like this. It is best to start slowly and then build up your speed to gather momentum to throw the loop

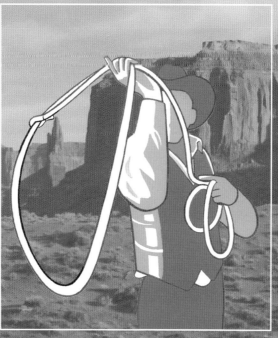

12 When you are ready to throw the rope, throw your right arm forward in a straight line and release the rope

FLAT SPIN

① Hold the loop of the rope and the end of the Spoke together in your right hand. With your left hand hold the rope between your thumb and index finger

② Bring your right arm back and your left arm across, so that the rope is held at your side. Swing the rope around in front of you

③ As the rope comes out in front of you, release the rope from your left hand

④ When the Honda has swung round 180 degrees in front of you, release the Spoke so that you are left holding just the end of the rope

⑤ Swing the rope around in a circular motion using the whole of your arm

⑥ As the rope spins around, spin your thumb and index finger to stop the rope from twisting

WEDDING RING

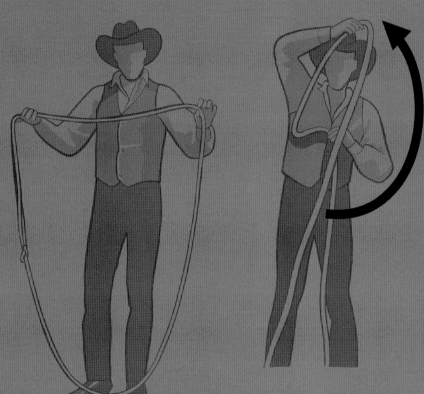

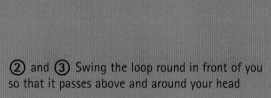

② and ③ Swing the loop round in front of you so that it passes above and around your head

① Hold the rope the same as for a Flat Spin, with the loop of the rope and the end of the Spoke together in your right hand. With your left hand hold the rope between your thumb and index finger

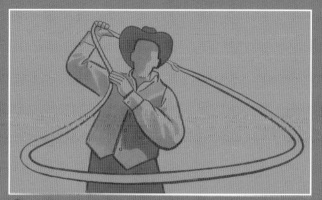

④ As the Honda moves behind your head, release the rope from your left hand

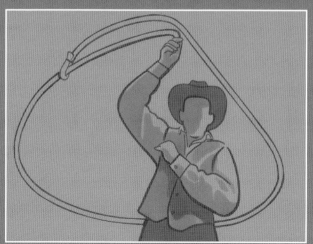

⑤ As the rope passes back in front of you, release the Spoke so that you are left holding just the end of the rope

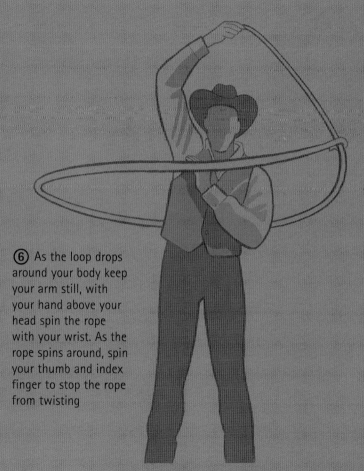

⑥ As the loop drops around your body keep your arm still, with your hand above your head spin the rope with your wrist. As the rope spins around, spin your thumb and index finger to stop the rope from twisting

JUGGLING & PEN SPINNING

THE ART OF JUGGLING IS USUALLY ASSOCIATED WITH CIRCUS PERFORMERS AND GOES BACK CENTURIES. IN FRONT OF AN AUDIENCE, JUGGLING MAY WELL BE PRESENTED AS A COMEDY ACT, HAPHAZARD BEHAVIOR MASKING THE SKILL IT TAKES TO NEARLY DROP THE ITEMS BEING JUGGLED.

In addition to the element of showmanship, juggling can be a relaxing pastime and help to improve hand to eye coordination. With the added bonus of causing the performer to look extremely cool.

Accomplished performers regularly look for more exotic items to juggle to increase their prowess with an audience. Flaming torches are common, even chainsaws are not unknown. In the hands of the novice, however, an acceptance of the adage "walk before you run" is a good survival tip.

When learning, find something you are comfortable handling, preferably not perishable items that will make a mess or be rendered inedible when dropped—something which is going to happen frequently at first. Beanbags are ideal as they are easy to catch and will not roll away. Juggling requires space so make sure there is nothing around you that could get damaged, or damage you, should you make contact with it.

Pen spinning is a form of "contact juggling" (also known as "object manipulation"), whereby the object(s) being juggled stay in contact with the body while they are being maneuvered. Many people indulge in this activity without knowing it, we often see people spinning during a tedious meeting or seminar, flipping a pen around the thumb, using the forefinger.

While many items, not just pens, can be used for spinning there is not currently a market for professional supplies. Accomplished spinners have begun to modify their pens to improve balance and maneuverability in order to facilitate ever more complex tricks. There does not appear to be a governing body associated with pen spinning that dictates rules regarding such modifications affecting the purity of the discipline.

For the amateur wishing to achieve notoriety as a pen spinner, it is advisable to begin with a more benign writing implement such as an unsharpened pencil. This will avoid accidental jabs to the hand and getting covered in ink marks. Practising can take place almost anywhere, though it may be advisable to conduct this activity in private rather than in an environment where you are supposed to be paying attention and using your pen in the manner for which it was intended. At least until a level of effortless proficiency has been reached.

ONE BALL

START BY USING JUST ONE BALL TO GET USED TO THE BASIC STANCE AND MOVES AND ALWAYS AIM NOT TO RUSH YOUR THROWING. THROW THE BALL IN A GOOD, STEADY RHYTHM AS THIS GIVES YOU MORE TIME TO COMPLETE EACH ACTION.

① Stand with your feet shoulder width apart, your hands horizontally out in front of you and the ball held in your favored hand (i.e. your right hand if you are right-handed). Focus your eyes on an imaginary point just above your horizontal eye-line

② Throw the ball up so that it just passes above the point on which your eyes are focused. Keep your eyes focused on that same point, *do not* follow the flight of the ball with your eyes

③ Catch the ball in your other hand (your off hand). Throw the ball back up, as before, and catch it in your favored hand. Continue to throw the ball from hand to hand in this fashion until you are confident with it.

TWO BALLS

② Throw one of the balls in your favored hand first. As this ball passes the point on which your eyes are focused begin to throw the ball in your other hand up

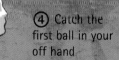

① Stand as before, but with one ball in each hand

④ Catch the first ball in your off hand

③ Keep your eyes focused on that same point, do *not* follow the flight of the balls with your eyes

⑤ Catch the second ball in your favored hand. Continue to practice this way until you are confident with it. Then repeat the process but start by throwing first from your off hand until you are also confident doing it that way

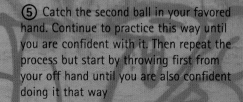

THREE BALL CASCADE

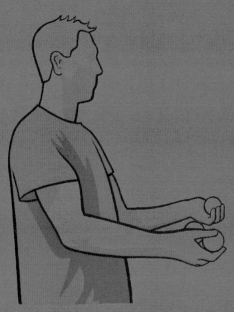

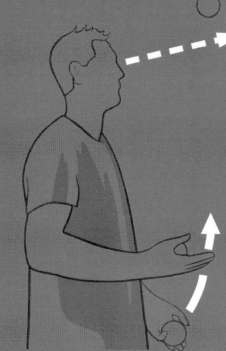

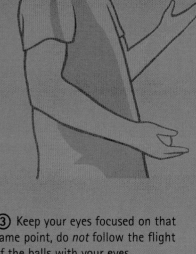

① Stand as before, but with two balls in your favored hand and one in your off hand

② Throw one of the balls in your favored hand first. As this ball passes the point on which your eyes are focused begin to throw the ball in your other hand up

③ Keep your eyes focused on that same point, do *not* follow the flight of the balls with your eyes

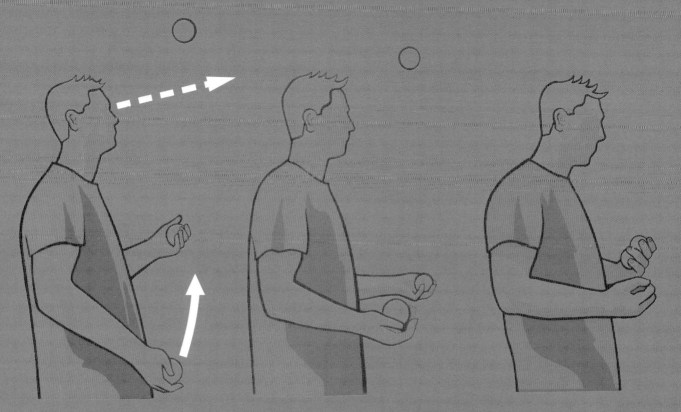

④ Catch the first ball in your off hand. As the second ball passes the point on which your eyes are focused begin to throw the third ball (the second ball in your favored hand) up

⑤ Catch the second ball in your favored hand

⑥ Catch the third ball in your off hand. Continue to practice this way until you are confident with it. Then repeat the process but start with two balls in your off hand until you are also confident doing it that way. Once you are confident starting with either hand continue throwing the balls rather than stopping once you have initially thrown and caught all three.

360° FORWARD SPIN

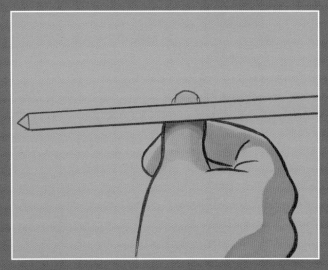

① Find the centre of gravity of the pen by balancing it on the back of your thumb

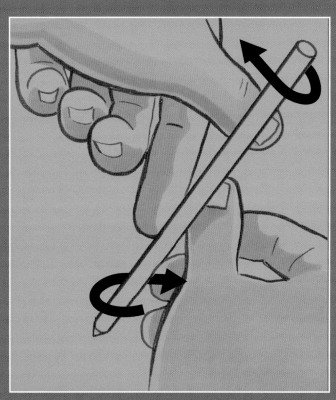

② Roll the pen around your thumb to the start position

BLOCKING FINGER

PUSHING FINGER

CATCHING FINGER

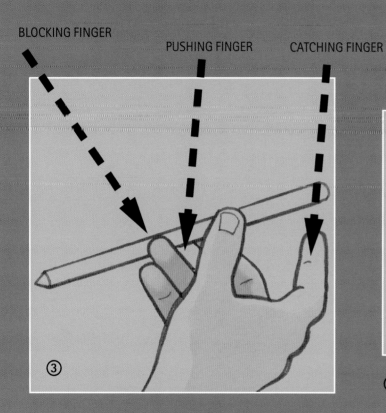

③

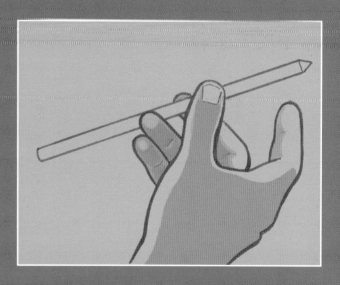

④ Start the trick with the pen held like this

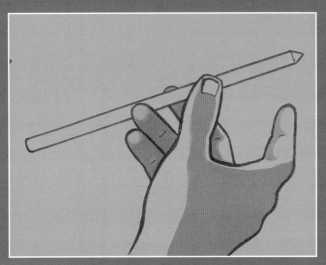

⑤ Begin by pushing the pen round with your pushing finger

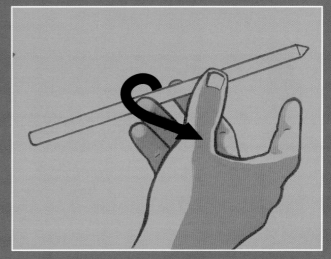

⑥ Move your blocking finger down, out of the path of the pen

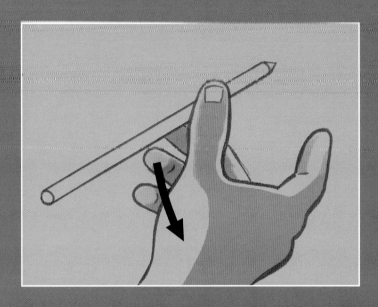

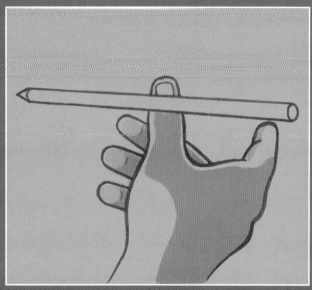

⑦ Keep your thumb straight and your catching finger out of the way as the pen spins around

⑧ Half way through the trick the pen is rotating on the center of gravity you found earlier

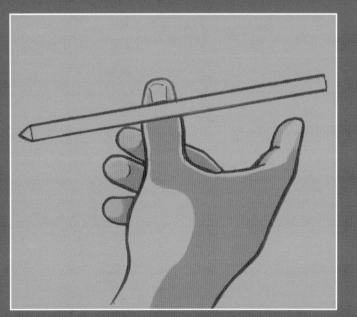 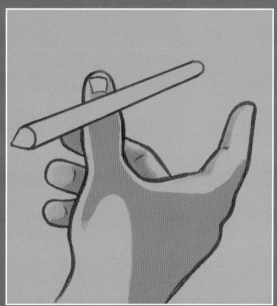

⑨ and ⑩ Continue to keep your thumb straight and your catching finger out of the way as the pen spins around

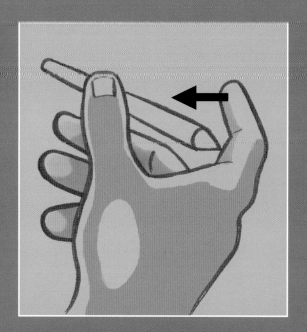

⑪ Once the pen has spun past your catching finger begin to bring your catching finger in

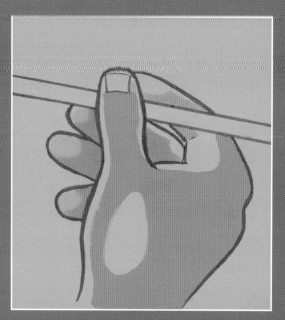

⑫ Catch the pen between your thumb and your catching finger

360° REVERSE SPIN

CATCHING FINGER   PUSHING FINGER

①

② Start with your hand tilted slightly downward

③ Begin by pushing the pen round with your pushing finger in the opposite direction to the Forward Spin.

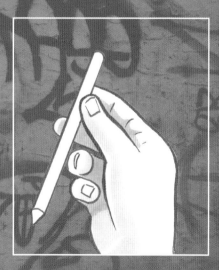

⑥ Catch the pen between your thumb and both your catching and pushing fingers

④ and ⑤ Keep your thumb straight as the pen spins around

● POOL

POOL, ALSO KNOWN AS EIGHT BALL, WAS INVENTED IN THE U.S. IN THE EARLY 1900S. THE BASIC RULES ARE SIMPLE. PLAYERS TAKE IT IN TURNS TO POT COLORED, NUMBERED BALLS (EITHER SPOTTED OR STRIPPED) FINISHING ON THE BLACK EIGHT BALL.

Although American Rules eight ball is played professionally all over the globe, the game also has myriad rules and governing bodies internationally. In the United Kingdom, for example, pool is often known as Black Ball.

Eight ball and pool halls have a strong influence in popular culture and are often featured as a plot device in film and TV. Phrases such as "Behind the eight ball" (finding oneself in a difficult position, from which there may be no escape) have entered colloquial English.

Playing pool for sport is all very well, but to really show flair you need to master some trick shots (known professionally as "Artistic Pool"). Fancy trick shot action has featured in a number of motion pictures, notably *The Hustler* (1961) and *The Color of Money* (1986), both starring Paul Newman. In both pictures, actors were able to be coached to perform almost all of the tricks required by the script. Accomplished trick shot professionals in the United States in particular enjoy a certain celebrity status.

Ball control is paramount when performing trick shots. There is much more to striking the cue ball onto the next, known as the "object ball":

- Draw—striking the cue ball at its base will create backspin, once it has hit the object ball it will roll back toward you.
- Topspin—achieved by striking the cue ball above center and following through with the cue. This will give extra momentum and enable the ball to roll through after the object ball.
- English—used to control the speed of the cue ball after it strikes the object ball. Achieved by striking the cue ball at the left or right hand side, causing it to spin.
- Chalking—enables the "tip" of the cue to grip the surface of the cue ball as it strikes. Without chalk, the cue ball will slip. Ideally the tip of the cue should be chalked before every shot.

TRICK SHOT POOL PLAYERS OF NOTE:

Mike Massey (U.S.)—2006 Trick Shot Magic Champion, author and instructor.
Andy "The Magic Man" Segal—2007 World Artistic Pool Champion, holds the current world record for fastest fifteen ball rack run (as of 2007).
Sebastian Giumelli (South America)—2007 South American Trick Shot Champion.

STRIKING THE CUE BALL

Follow (also known as Topspin), causes the cue ball to follow through more than usual after it has struck a ball

Left English (also known as Left Sidespin), will cause the cue ball to travel slightly to the right of where it is aimed. On hitting another ball a cue ball struck with Left English will cause that ball to spin in the opposite direction to the cue ball. After striking a ball a cue ball struck with Left English will then spin to the left.

Right English (also known as Right Sidespin), will cause the cue ball to travel slightly to the left of where it is aimed. On hitting another ball a cue ball struck with Right English will cause that ball to spin in the opposite direction to the cue ball. After striking a ball a cue ball struck with Right English will then spin to the right.

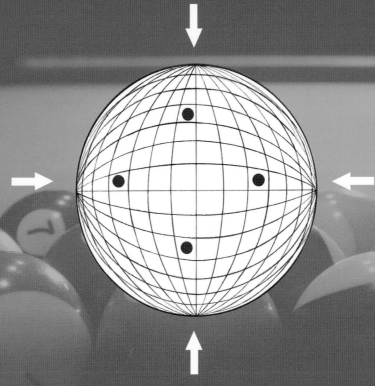

Draw (also known as Backspin), causes the cue ball to reverse back after it has struck a ball

SCATTER BREAK

THIS BREAK IS INTENDED TO SCATTER THE BALLS IN THE HOPE THAT
YOU WILL SINK AT LEAST ONE BALL DIRECTLY FROM THE BREAK

① Start with the cue ball ⅓ of the way across the table.
Strike the cue ball hard and aim for the center of the front
ball in the rack

② The balls will scatter around the table

8 BALL BREAK

THIS BREAK IS INTENDED TO SINK THE EIGHT
BALL DIRECTLY FROM THE BREAK

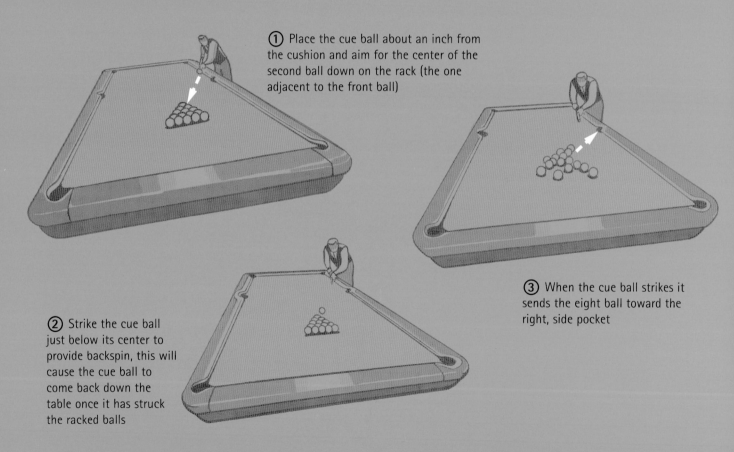

① Place the cue ball about an inch from
the cushion and aim for the center of the
second ball down on the rack (the one
adjacent to the front ball)

② Strike the cue ball
just below its center to
provide backspin, this will
cause the cue ball to
come back down the
table once it has struck
the racked balls

③ When the cue ball strikes it
sends the eight ball toward the
right, side pocket

9 BALL BREAK

THIS BREAK IS INTENDED TO SCATTER THE
BALLS IN THE HOPE THAT YOU WILL SINK AT
LEAST ONE BALL DIRECTLY FROM THE BREAK
IN A GAME OF NINE BALL

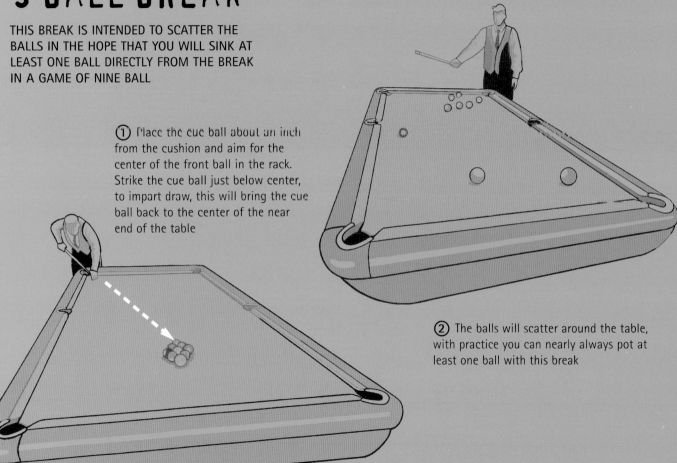

① Place the cue ball about an inch
from the cushion and aim for the
center of the front ball in the rack.
Strike the cue ball just below center,
to impart draw, this will bring the cue
ball back to the center of the near
end of the table

② The balls will scatter around the table,
with practice you can nearly always pot at
least one ball with this break

INVERTED SPIN BANK SHOT

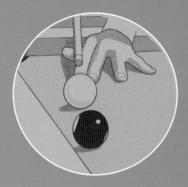

① Aim the cue ball slightly to the right of center of the eight ball

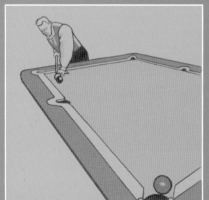

② Strike the cue ball, applying left English. This will impart left English to the eight ball

③ and ④ The eight ball will travel down the table and strike the far cushion to the left of the far right pocket

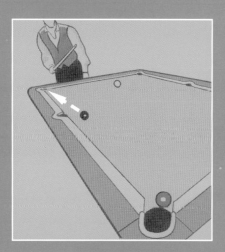

5 and **6** When the eight ball strikes the far cushion the spin imparted to it will cause it to spin back up the table and curve back toward the near right pocket

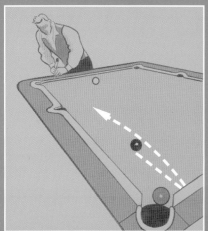

7 The eight ball drops into the near right pocket

THREE CUSHION BANK SHOT

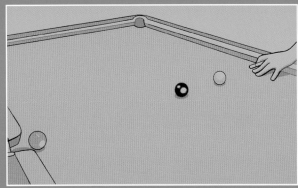

① Set the balls up as shown. Aim the cue ball to strike the eight ball slightly on the right, this will impart Right English to the eight ball

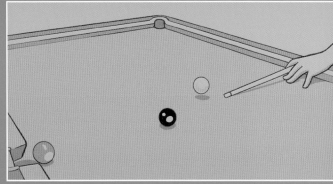

② Strike the cue ball slightly to the left, to impart Left English to it. This will increase the right English imparted to the eight ball

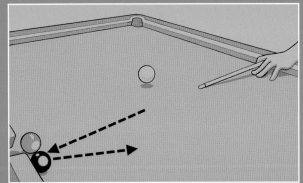

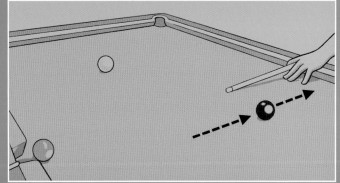

③ and ④ The eight ball strikes the cushion and heads across and down the table

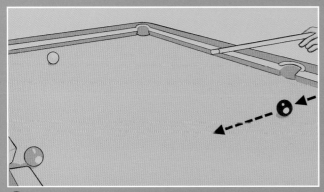

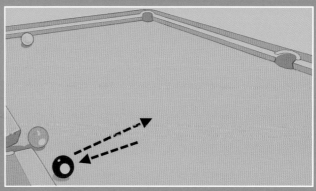

⑤ The eight ball strikes the cushion and heads across and back up the table

⑥ The eight ball strikes the cushion and heads across and back up the table toward the middle pocket

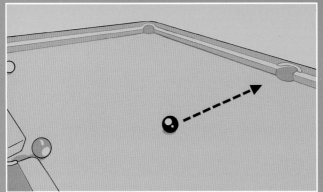

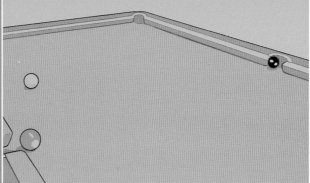

⑦ and ⑧ The eight ball will drop into the nearside middle pocket

SWERVE SHOT

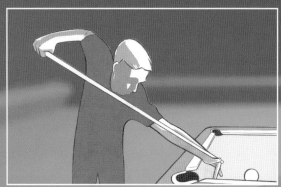

① Hold the cue at a 45 degree angle

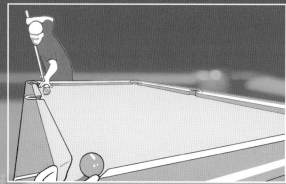

② Strike the cue ball, applying Right English and a little Draw. Don't strike the cue ball too hard as this will cause it to curve too late and therefore miss the target ball. Likewise if you strike the cue ball too softly it will curve too soon and miss the target ball

③ On being struck, the cue ball will jump up slightly and begin to curve around the first ball

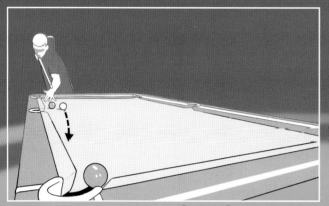 

④ and ⑤ The cue ball will curve back in toward the cushion

⑥ The cue ball will strike the cushion and head down the table

⑦ The cue ball will strike the target ball and sink it in the pocket

YO-YO

EVER THE POPULAR MAINSTAY OF SCHOOLYARD PURSUITS, "YO-YOING" IS A GREAT WAY TO IMPRESS FRIENDS AND POTENTIAL ADMIRERS WITH YOUR MANUAL DEXTERITY WITHOUT THE NEED TO VAST AREAS OF OPEN SPACE, EQUIPMENT OR A TEAM OF PARTICIPANTS

Supposedly invented as a weapon, the origins of the yo-yo can be traced back through many hundreds of years of human culture across the globe. Though of course, most people pick one up to look cool and maybe get girls.

Originally yo-yos were made of wood, but as technology and player skill advanced, this was discarded in favor of plastic or aluminum. Variations in wood's natural make up cause weight fluctuations which can become an issue if you want your yo-yo to do more than just go up and down. More exotic materials and mechanisms are used by top level players.

Although yo-yoing does not enjoy as high a profile as other alternative sports, the yo-yo has about as dedicated a following of enthusiasts as you could hope to get. The sport is incredibly popular in Japan, which along with the United States has produced some of the world's greatest players. Competitive events are very audience-friendly. Freestyle routines are usually set to music which serves as a guide for competitors to follow. So called "ladder" competitions involve a series of progressively difficult tricks.

Yo-yoing, basic technique:

- Stringing is a vital element in successful yo-yoing. The length of string should be tailored to your height; too long and your yo-yo will keep hitting the floor. Trim the string to the length required and tie the end in a slipknot. Place the loop of the slipknot over at least the first knuckle of your middle finger to prevent it slipping off.
- A controlled but powerful throw is required for plenty of momentum. Hold the yo-yo in the palm facing up, curling the hand toward the wrist, bring it up close to your shoulder and straight back down again, allowing the yo-yo to roll forward from your hand. If you have provided enough force the yo-yo will stay spinning at the end of the string, turning your hand over should make it shoot back up into your palm—simple!
- Remember to give yourself plenty of room, the last thing you need is the yo-yo smashing straight through the TV screen, making unsightly marks on the ceiling, or, even giving the dog a black eye...

YO-YO PLAYERS OF NOTE:

Yuuki Spencer (U.S.)—2007 World Yo-Yo Contest 1A Division 1st place.
Hiroyuki Suzuki (Japan)—2007 World Yo-Yo Contest 1A Division 2nd Place.
Steve Brown (U.S.)—"Drunken Yo-Yo" performer and yo-yo innovator.

FORWARD PASS

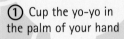
① Cup the yo-yo in the palm of your hand

② Throw your arm forward, quickly but smoothly. When your arm reaches 90 degrees to your chest flick your wrist forward, ensure that you throw the yo-yo in a straight line

③ Make sure that the yo-yo extends all the way to the end of the string

④ When the string is fully
extended flick your wrist around
180 degrees so that your hand is
facing palm upwards

⑤ Catch the yo-yo as
it returns to your hand

SLEEPER

BEFORE BEGINNING THE SLEEPER YOU WILL NEED TO REDUCE THE TENSION OF YOUR STRING. UNWIND YOUR YO-YO COMPLETELY AND LET THE BODY SPIN UNTIL IT COMES TO A NATURAL STOP

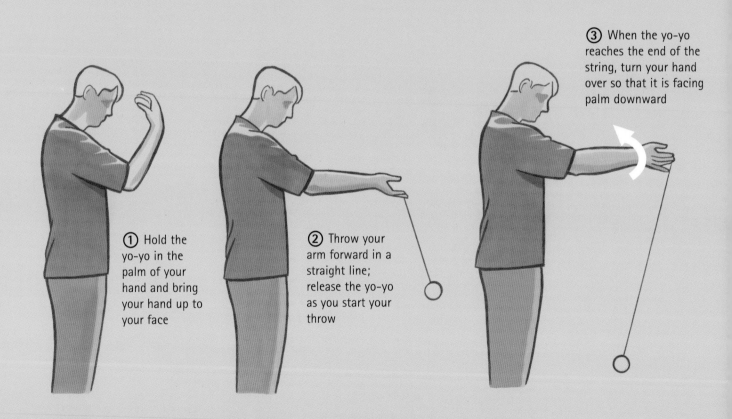

① Hold the yo-yo in the palm of your hand and bring your hand up to your face

② Throw your arm forward in a straight line; release the yo-yo as you start your throw

③ When the yo-yo reaches the end of the string, turn your hand over so that it is facing palm downward

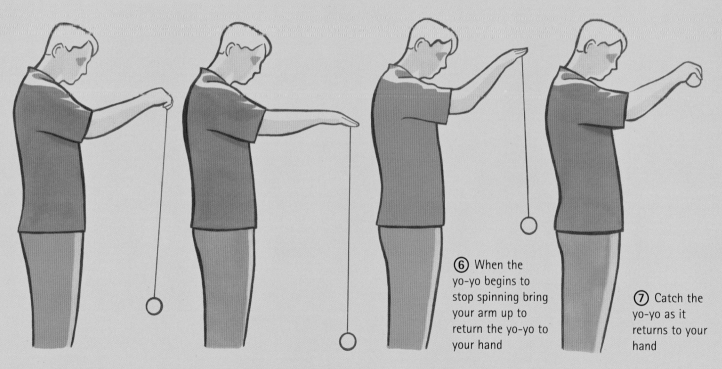

④ and ⑤ The yo-yo will spin at the end of the string for a few moments

⑥ When the yo-yo begins to stop spinning bring your arm up to return the yo-yo to your hand

⑦ Catch the yo-yo as it returns to your hand

FLYING SAUCER

NOT ONLY DOES THE FLYING SAUCER TRICK LOOK GREAT, IT CAN ALSO BE USED TO LOOSEN THE STRING OF YOUR YO-YO IF IT HAS BECOME TOO TIGHT, OR TIGHTEN IT IF IT HAS BECOME TOO LOOSE (THROW THE YO-YO TO THE LEFT TO LOOSEN AND THE RIGHT TO TIGHTEN THE STRING).

① Cup the yo-yo in the palm of your right hand, with your arm held at a slight angle away from your body

② Throw your arm diagonally across your body; release the yo-yo as you start your throw

③ Turn your wrist 90 degrees, so that your palm is facing your stomach. Hold your hand steady

④ The yo-yo will sleep for a moment and then begin to bounce up and down and spin

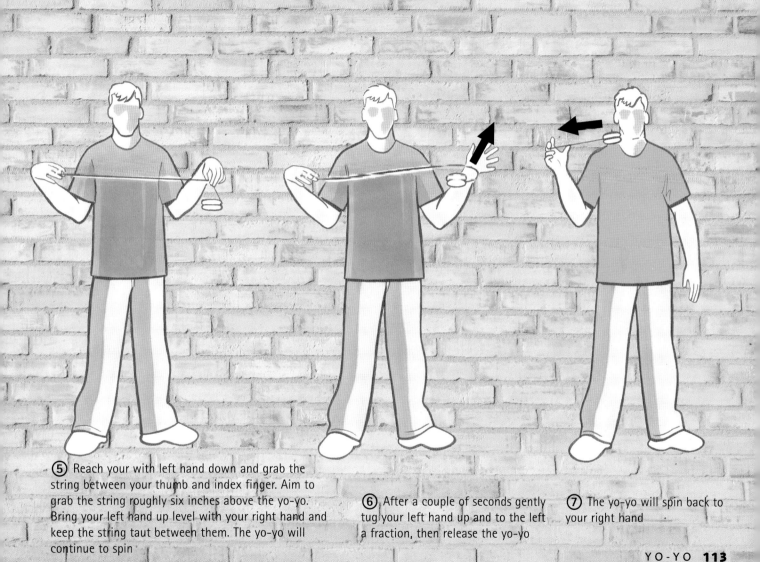

⑤ Reach your with left hand down and grab the string between your thumb and index finger. Aim to grab the string roughly six inches above the yo-yo. Bring your left hand up level with your right hand and keep the string taut between them. The yo-yo will continue to spin

⑥ After a couple of seconds gently tug your left hand up and to the left a fraction, then release the yo-yo

⑦ The yo-yo will spin back to your right hand

AROUND THE WORLD

① Cup the yo-yo in the palm of your hand

② Throw your arm forward, quickly but smoothly. When your arm reaches 90 degrees to your chest flick your wrist forward, the same as for a Forward Pass

③ Make sure that the yo-yo extends all the way to the end of the string

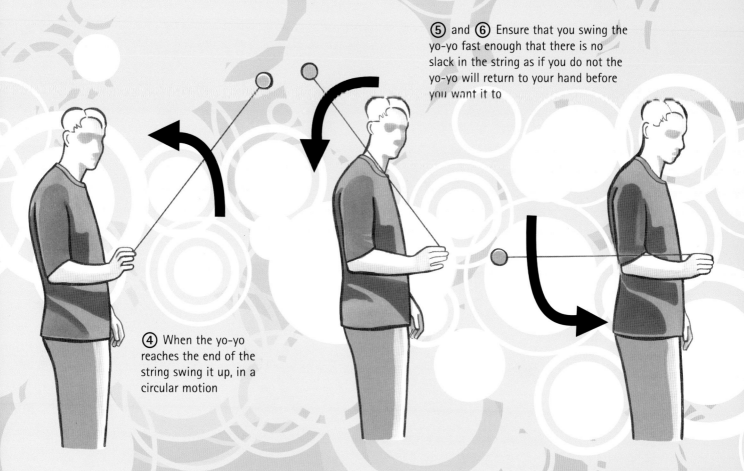

⑤ and ⑥ Ensure that you swing the yo-yo fast enough that there is no slack in the string as if you do not the yo-yo will return to your hand before you want it to

④ When the yo-yo reaches the end of the string swing it up, in a circular motion

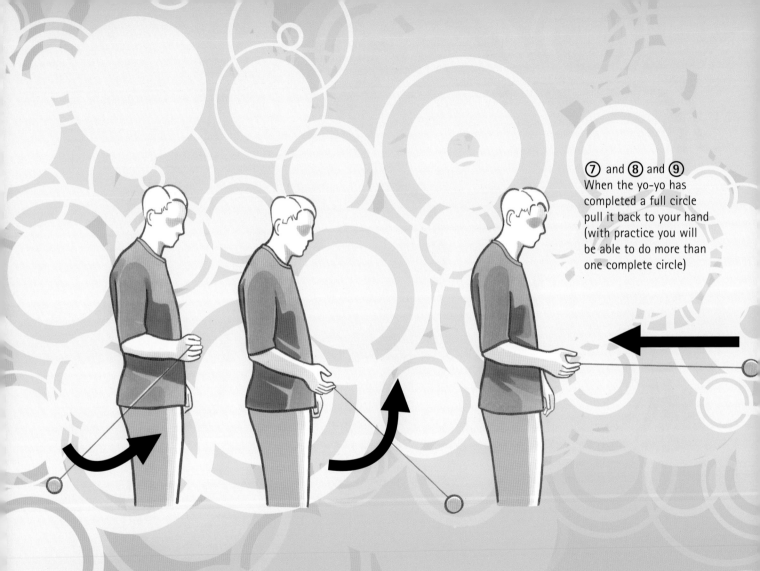

7 and 8 and 9
When the yo-yo has completed a full circle pull it back to your hand (with practice you will be able to do more than one complete circle)

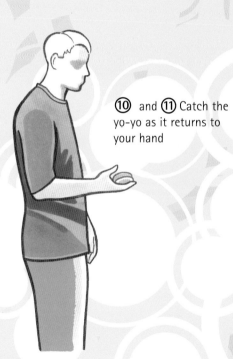

⑩ and ⑪ Catch the yo-yo as it returns to your hand

TRAPEZE

① Hold the yo-yo between your thumb and index finger. Bring your arm up at your side, level with your shoulder

② Throw your arm down and across in front of you

③ As the yo-yo swings down, bring your left arm up and point forward with your index finger

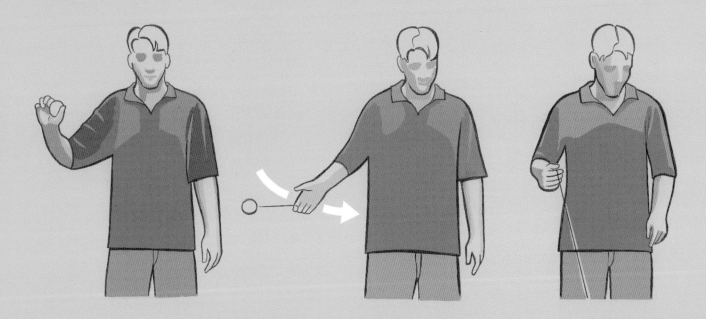

④ As the yo-yo comes into contact with your index finger, slide your index finger along the string from right to left.

⑤ and ⑥ The yo-yo will swing around your index finger 180 degrees and land back on the string. The yo-yo will spin on the string for a few moments.

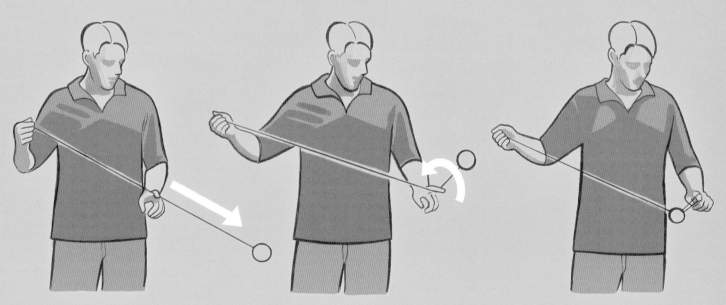

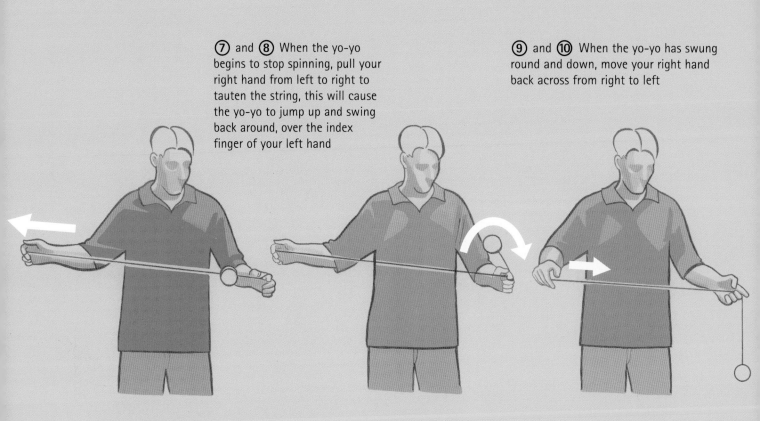

7 and **8** When the yo-yo begins to stop spinning, pull your right hand from left to right to tauten the string, this will cause the yo-yo to jump up and swing back around, over the index finger of your left hand

9 and **10** When the yo-yo has swung round and down, move your right hand back across from right to left

⑪ and **⑫** When the yo-yo string is fully extended, lift your right arm up to head height. Just before your right hand reaches head height, move your left hand from right to left. This will cause the yo-yo to loop back over

⑬ and **⑭** and **⑮** The momentum of the yo-yo will cause it to drop down slightly

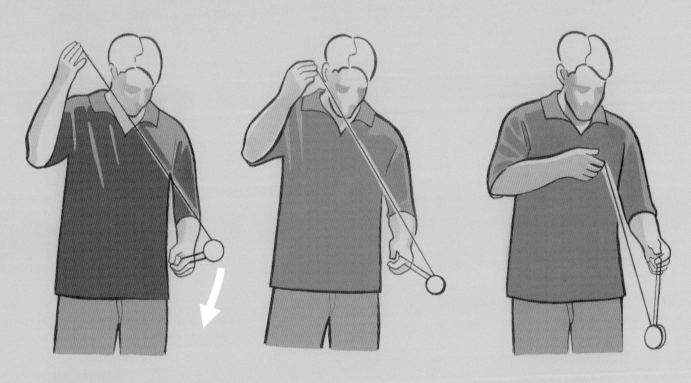

(16) and (17) and (18) When the yo-yo has spun for a moment, release the string from your left hand and give the string in your right hand a slight tug upward. The yo-yo will return to your right hand

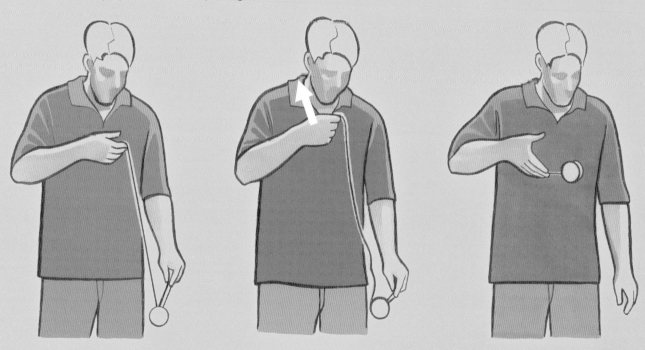

ELEVATOR

① Cup the yo-yo in the palm of your hand and bring your hand up to your face

② Throw your arm forward in a straight line; release the yo-yo as you start your throw

③ and ④ Bring your left arm forward and extend the index finger of your left hand

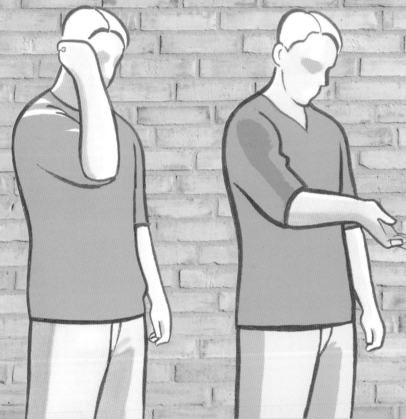

⑤ and ⑥ Raise your left hand up so that the yo-yo comes back up and begins to spin on the string

⑦ and ⑧ Move your right hand gently down, the yo-yo will rise up the string

⑨ Once the yo-yo has reached your left hand, bring your right hand back up gently. The yo-yo will come back down toward your right hand

⑩ and ⑪ Move your left hand down, the yo-yo will come away from the string and drop down

⑫ When the yo-yo string is fully extended, raise your right hand and bring your left hand into the string, with your index finger extended

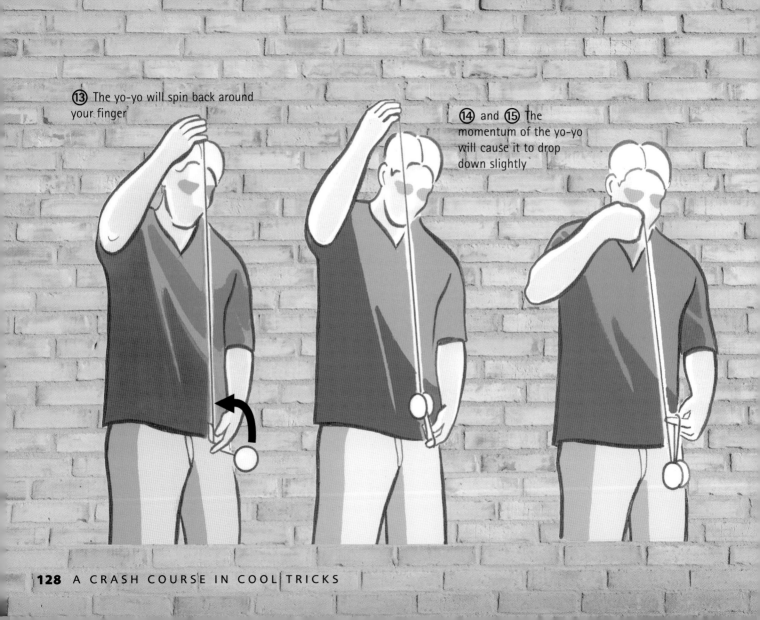

(13) The yo-yo will spin back around your finger

(14) and (15) The momentum of the yo-yo will cause it to drop down slightly

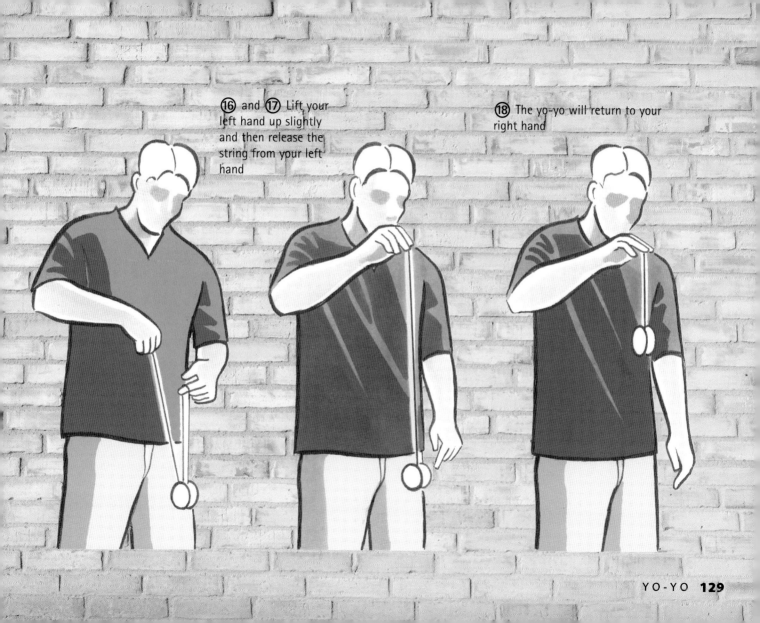

⑯ and ⑰ Lift your left hand up slightly and then release the string from your left hand

⑱ The yo-yo will return to your right hand

CARD SHUFFLING

THE PURPOSE OF SHUFFLING A DECK OF CARDS IS TO RANDOMIZE THEM READY FOR PLAY. MACHINES HAVE BEEN DEVISED TO DO THE JOB TO REMOVE THE POSSIBILITY OF CHEATING, BUT WHO WANTS TO WATCH A GRACELESS BOX DO THE JOB WHEN A MUNDANE TASK CAN BE TURNED INTO SOMETHING BEAUTIFUL?

Few scenes in cinematic history evoke more nostalgia than James Bond striding into a casino, ordering a Vodka Martini (shaken, not stirred, obviously) before sitting down to enjoy a few hands of his favourite game, Baccarat. OK, so Bond seems to favor Texas Holdem these days during those dull moments between saving the world and practicing the art of seduction, but one element of this scene remains constant—the effortless ease and cool exhibited by the dealer, or croupier, as he or she deftly shuffles the cards, their gaze never leaving that of our hero.

The art of shuffling cards is not one confined to the casino professional. In Poker, where projecting a confident, unruffled image is vital, players will routinely be called on for their turn to shuffle and deal, so it certainly pays to be able to wield the cards with precision and dexterity.

Learning to shuffle with panache is the first step on the road to "card manipulation", the art of using cards to perform magic tricks and sleight of hand. Recently "Extreme Card Manipulation" (XCM) has emerged, which has been likened to the freestyle elements of sports such as skateboarding. Extreme Card Manipulators develop their own tricks and techniques with numerous books and DVDs available on the subject.

A playing card is not just a playing card. Professional card manipulators are known to favor those embossed with tiny, raised dimples on the surface of the card, known as an "air cushion". This allows the cards to glide more smoothly across each other. A "Linoid" finish incorporates an extra coating to help prevent the cards picking up grease and grime. This also makes the card extra stiff. Cards that have a woven texture on the surface are finished in Cambric, a cotton fibre making them both hardwearing and easier to handle. The type used is purely down to personal preference.

Top tips to successful shuffling:

- Start slowly, good shuffling takes practice. Take things a step at a time and your speed will quickly increase.
- If you are using a new deck you may find the cards too firm, making them difficult to shuffle. Break them in by gently bending back and forth.
- As you gain experience, try a different type of deck to see how it affects your technique.

RIFFLE SHUFFLE

① Separate the deck into two equal halves (with practice you will be able to do this by feel alone)

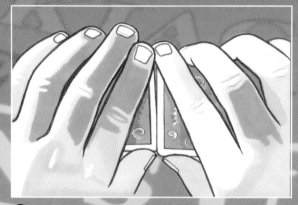

② Place your hands on the two halves of the deck with your index fingers pressing down on the front corner of each half and your thumbs at the back corner of each half

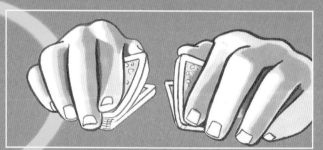

③ Move the two half decks so that they form a V. With your thumbs, lift the back corners up about an inch

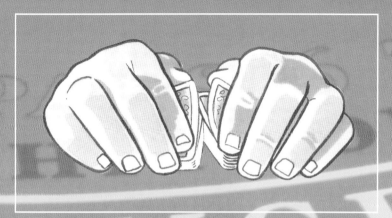

④ With your thumbs, riffle the two half decks together so that they mix together

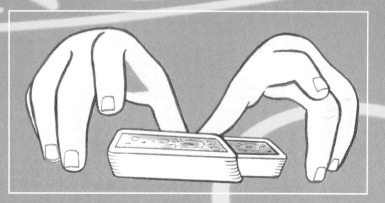

⑤ Push the two intermingled half decks together

BUTTERFLY SHUFFLE

① Hold the deck as if you were about to deal and riffle the cards until you are halfway through the deck

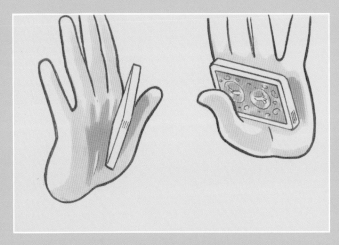

② Place one half of the deck in each hand so that the cards are held between the base of your thumb and the palm of your hand

③ Riffle the two half decks together using the little fingers of each hand

④ Push the two intermingled half decks together

FANS

PRACTICE MAKING FANS WITH JUST TWO CARDS, AS YOU BECOME MORE PROFICIENT BUILD UP THE NUMBER OF CARDS UNTIL YOU CAN DO A HALF DECK IN EACH HAND.

① Hold the cards with three fingers on the back

② Your thumb should be just off center, on the bottom left hand side as you look at the cards

③ Fan the cards out by moving your thumb in a semi-circular motion across the base of the cards while holding them with the three fingers behind the deck

④ You should be able to see each card once you have completed the fan

RIBBON SPREAD

① Hold the deck face up, with your thumb at the base of the deck and your index finger to the side, just above halfway up the side of the deck

② Press down with your index finger and begin to fan the cards out from left to right. Use your thumb as a guide to decide the shape of the arc that you make with the deck as the cards fan out

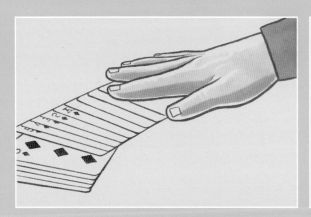

③ The harder you press down with your index finger the closer together the cards will be as you fan them out

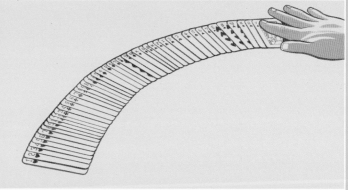

④ Keep your index finger pressed down on the cards until they are all spread out

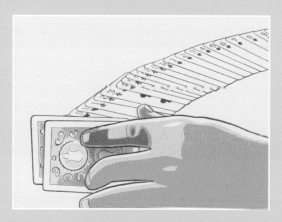

⑤ Lift the left hand end of the fanned out deck up until it is at a 90 degree angle to the table

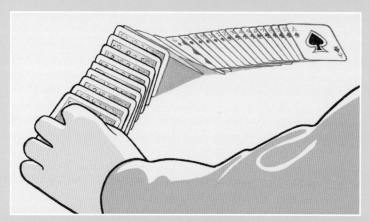

⑥ Flick the cards with your index finger so that they begin to tumble from left to right

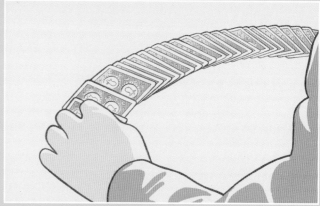

⑦ The deck will end up fanned out, face down on the table

ONE HANDED CUT

① Hold the deck
face down, so that
it is held in place
on all four sides

② Push up half of
the deck with your
thumb and move
your index finger
back to release the
bottom half of the
deck

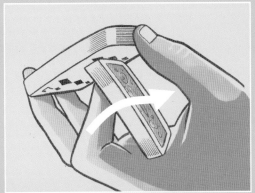

③ Push your index finger in, back toward your
thumb. Do *not* push your index finger upward as
this will cause the cards to fall

④ The top half of the deck will now fall into place and
become the bottom half

ONE HANDED DEAL

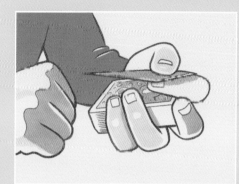

① Push the top card forward with your thumb and slide your index finger under the card

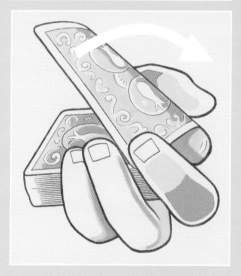

② Bring your middle finger round and use it to lever the card forward

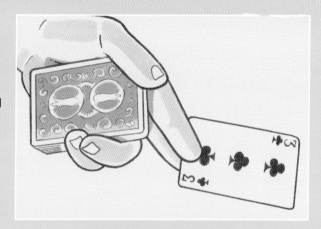

③ Flip the card over and, holding it between your index finger and your middle finger, place it on the table

PAPER PLANES

THE SKILLS REQUIRED TO PERFECT PAPER PLANE CONSTRUCTION ARE NOT TOO FAR REMOVED FROM THOSE OF ORIGAMI (FROM THE JAPANESE WORDS "ORU" MEANING PAPER AND "KAMI" MEANING TO FOLD). HOWEVER, WHILE ORIGAMI CAN BE TRACED BACK THROUGH THE ANNALS OF TIME TO WHEN PAPER PRODUCTION AND FOLDING TECHNIQUES WERE INTRODUCED TO THE COUNTRY FROM CHINA, THE ORIGINS OF PAPER PLANES ARE LESS CLEAR.

Of course, flying paper creations such as kites and hot air balloons have been around for centuries. But there is some debate about when paper planes began to be popularized, after all, aircraft are a relatively new development, so paper planes imitating them cannot pre-date this point in history. It would seem to be around the early part of the 20th century that paper plane creation began in earnest.

Principally, paper planes were used to test the aerodynamics of full-size aircraft. Jack Northrop, cofounder of the American Lockheed Corporation, used them to test wing design. While Englishman A.V. Roe, before starting AVRO & Co (responsible for the British WWII Lancaster bomber), designed and built paper models. Who knows, maybe even Wilbur and Orville Wright experimented with paper planes before making the world's first powered flight.

Purists argue that there should be no glue or sticky tape used in paper plane construction, nor should any weights (such as paper clips) or cuts in the flight surfaces be utilized. They should also be constructed from a single piece of paper. This leaves flight characteristics completely at the mercy of the maker's folding accuracy. Many planes with the fold lines can be conveniently printed or photocopied but for greater wow factor, learn the designs and construct them from memory.

Throwing a paper plane requires practice too. The amount of force required to launch your plane will vary according to its design while wind conditions should also be taken into account. To launch, hold the plane between your thumb and forefinger, draw your arm back and bring it forward slowly but firmly. Try to aim the plane at a 45 degree angle to give it some lift. Some practice will be required to get your plane launched consistently. Do try to make sure that there is no-one in the flight path, being struck in the eye by a paper plane is no joke!

PAPER PLANE INNOVATIONS AND INNOVATORS:

Ken Blackburn, aerospace engineer, currently holds the world record for paper plane flight at 27.6 seconds. The attempt took six months of preparation and training. Blackburn has also written four books on paper plane construction, making him something of an expert in the field.
If launching your plane seems to be simply too much effort, a battery powered launcher kit is available.

DART

THE DART IS AN IMPROVEMENT ON THE
BASIC PAPER PLANE THAT WE ALL LEARNED
TO MAKE AT SCHOOL

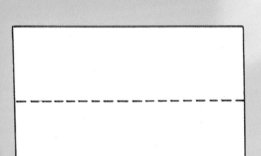

① Fold a standard Letter size piece of
paper and fold it in half horizontally

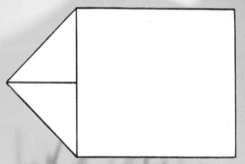

② Fold the left hand corners in so that
they meet in the middle, along the fold you
have just made

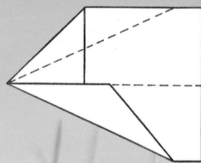

③ Fold the triangle that you have
just created into the middle again.

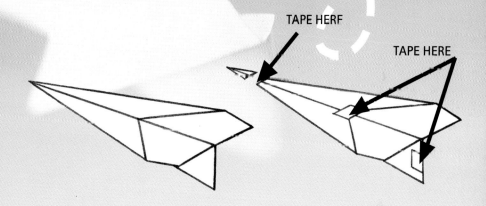

TAPE HERF

TAPE HERE

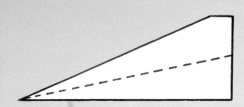

④ Fold the wings on either side down diagonally, along the dotted lines shown

⑤ Your Dart should look like this and is ready to fly

⑥ For added stability you can cut the nose of the plane off (roughly half an inch) and tape the front back and wings together. Only use a small amount of tape or you will unbalance the plane

ORIGAMI PLANE

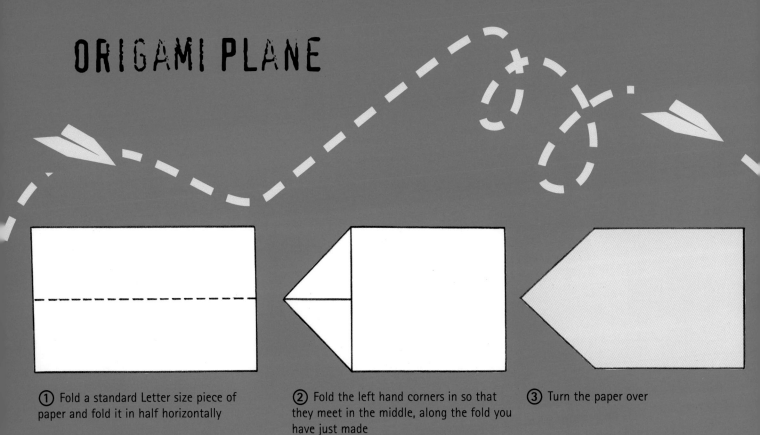

① Fold a standard Letter size piece of paper and fold it in half horizontally

② Fold the left hand corners in so that they meet in the middle, along the fold you have just made

③ Turn the paper over

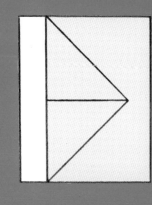

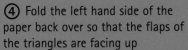

④ Fold the left hand side of the paper back over so that the flaps of the triangles are facing up

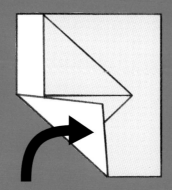

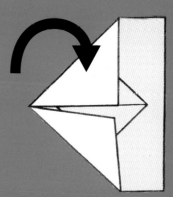

⑤ and ⑥ Fold the fold of the left hand corners in so that they meet in the middle, this will leave a tip of roughly one inch visible

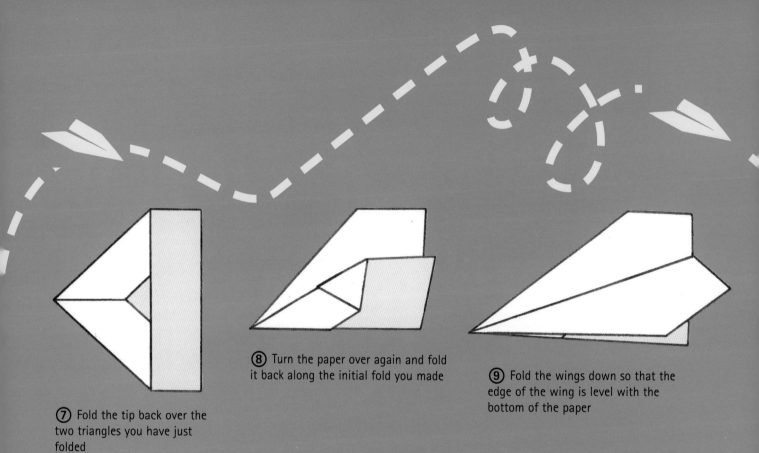

⑦ Fold the tip back over the two triangles you have just folded

⑧ Turn the paper over again and fold it back along the initial fold you made

⑨ Fold the wings down so that the edge of the wing is level with the bottom of the paper

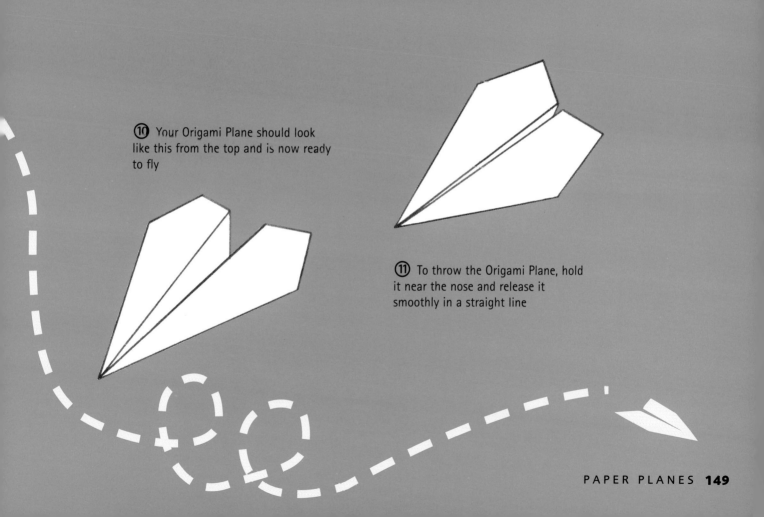

10 Your Origami Plane should look like this from the top and is now ready to fly

11 To throw the Origami Plane, hold it near the nose and release it smoothly in a straight line

SABERTOOTH

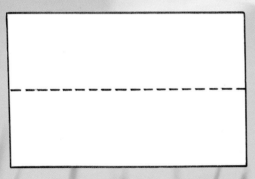

① Fold a standard Letter size piece of paper and fold it in half horizontally

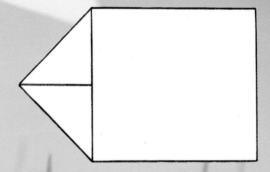

② Fold the left hand corners in so that they meet in the middle, along the fold you have just made

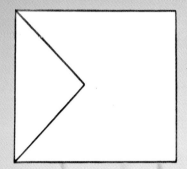

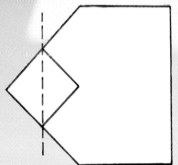

③ Fold the triangle this forms over to the right

④ and ⑤ Turn the paper over and make the same folds as in step two. Now turn the paper back over and fold the left triangle over so that it covers the right triangle

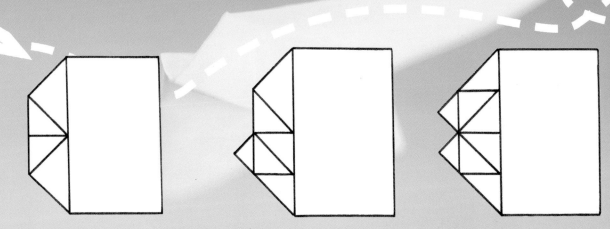

⑥ and ⑦ and ⑧ Turn the paper over again. Push the index finger of your right hand under the flap, this will raise the flap. Use your left hand to push the flap down and fold the paper so that you end up with step seven. Repeat this on the top flap to get step eight

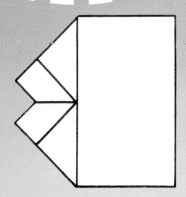

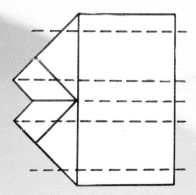

⑨ Turn the paper over again

⑩ and ⑪ Fold the paper along the lines shown in step ten so that face on your Sabertooth looks like step eleven

FLAPPER

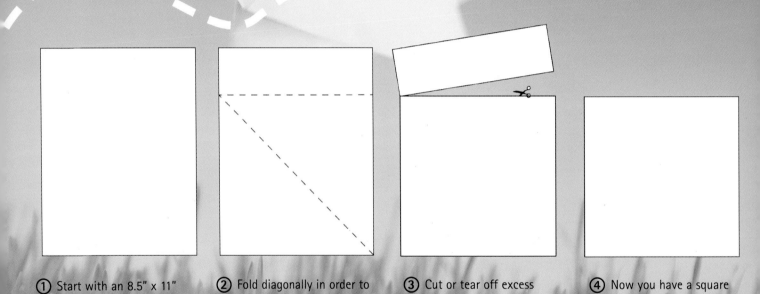

① Start with an 8.5" x 11" sheet of paper

② Fold diagonally in order to create a square

③ Cut or tear off excess

④ Now you have a square

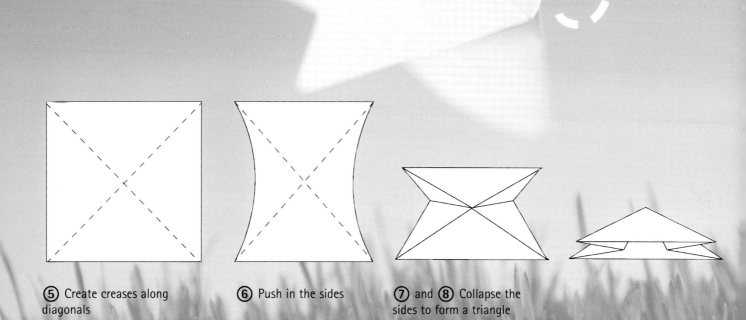

⑤ Create creases along diagonals

⑥ Push in the sides

⑦ and ⑧ Collapse the sides to form a triangle

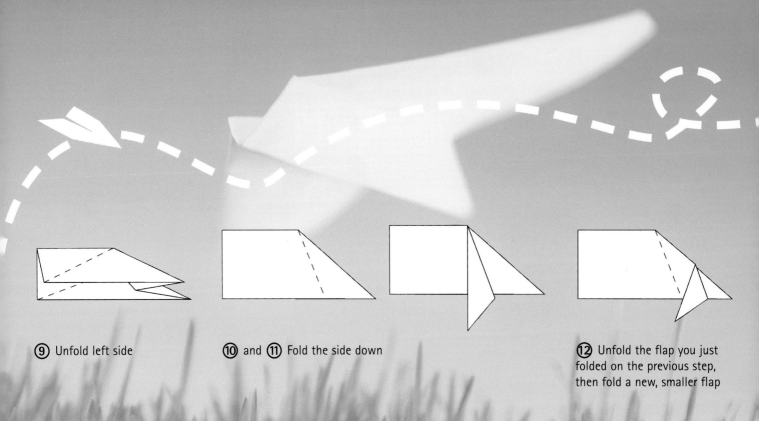

⑨ Unfold left side

⑩ and ⑪ Fold the side down

⑫ Unfold the flap you just folded on the previous step, then fold a new, smaller flap

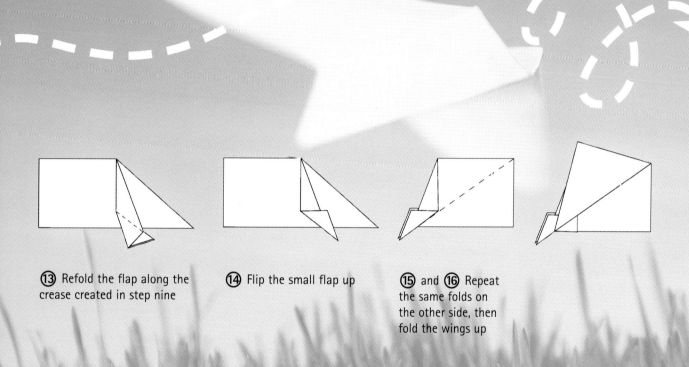

⑬ Refold the flap along the crease created in step nine

⑭ Flip the small flap up

⑮ and ⑯ Repeat the same folds on the other side, then fold the wings up

⑰ Turn flapper right side up

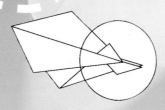

⑱ Now, to fold the front end...

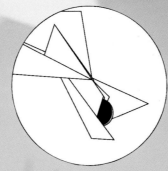

⑲ Place a small coin into one of the two slots at the front of the plane

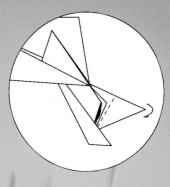

⑳ Fold right flap over the two slots (one of which has the small coin in it) and tuck inside

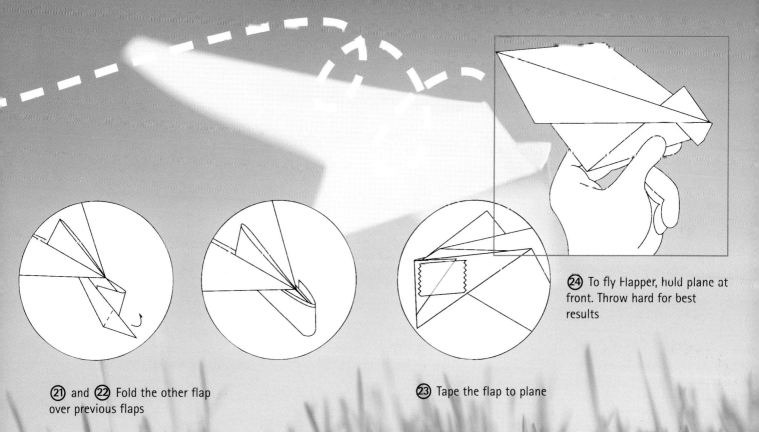

21 and **22** Fold the other flap over previous flaps

23 Tape the flap to plane

24 To fly Flapper, hold plane at front. Throw hard for best results

CREDITS

The Flapper paper plane was designed by Keith Greenstein and is, as far as we know, the only paper plane design that features flapping wings; our thanks to Keith for this great design.